POLITICAL REALITI
Edited on behalf of the
by Derek Heater

# The Cabinet and Policy Formation

Michael Rush

**Longman**
London and New York

LONGMAN GROUP LIMITED
*Longman House,*
*Burnt Mill, Harlow, Essex CM20 2JE, England*
*and Associated Companies throughout the World.*

Published in the United States of America by
Longman Inc., New York.

First published 1984
Second impression 1985
ISBN 0 582 36608 9 (cased)
ISBN 0 582 36619 4 (paper)

*Set in 10/12 Times Linotron 202*

*Produced by Longman Group (F.E.) Ltd.*
*Printed in Hong Kong*

---

**British Library Cataloguing in Publication Data**

Rush, Michael
    The cabinet and policy formation. – (Political
    realities)
    1. Great Britain – Cabinet
    I. Title    II. Series
    354.4104′09    JN401

    ISBN 0–582–36608–9
    ISBN 0–582–36619–4Pbk

---

**Library of Congress Cataloging in Publication Data**
Rush, Michael, 1937–
    The cabinet and policy formation.

    (Political realities)
    Bibliography: p.
    Includes index.
    1. Cabinet system – Great Britain.    I. Title.
II. Series.
JN405.R87 1983    320.441    83–9361
ISBN 0–582–36608–9
ISBN 0–582–36619–4 (pbk.)

# Contents

# Acknowledgements

We are grateful to the following for permission to reproduce copyright material:

Hamish Hamilton Ltd for extracts from *The Crossman Diaries: Diaries of a Cabinet Minister*, vols I, II & III by Richard Crossman, ed Janet Morgan, pub Hamish Hamilton Ltd/Jonathan Cape Ltd 1975, 1976 & 1977; Observer News Service for an extract from an article by Sir Alec Douglas Home from *The Observer* 23 August 1961; Times Newspapers Ltd for extracts from an article on Sir Harold Wilson by David Wood from *The Times* 3 March 1967.

# Political Realities: the Nature of the Series

A great need is felt for short books which can supplement or even replace textbooks and which can deal in an objective but realistic way with problems that arouse political controversy. The series aims to break from a purely descriptive and institutional approach to one that will show how and why there are different interpretations both of how things work and how they ought to work. Too often in the past 'British Constitution' has been taught quite apart from any knowledge of the actual political conflicts which institutions strive to contain. So the Politics Association continues to sponsor this now well-established series because it believes that a specifically civic education is an essential part of any liberal or general education, but that respect for political rules and an active citizenship can only be encouraged by helping pupils, students and young voters to discover what are the main objects of political controversy, the varying views about the nature of the constitution – themselves often highly political, and what are the most widely canvassed alternative policies in their society. From such a realistic appreciation of differences and conflicts reasoning can then follow about the common processes of containing or resolving them peacefully.

The specific topics chosen are based on an analysis of the main elements in existing A level syllabuses, and the manner in which they are treated is based on the conviction of the editors that almost every examination board has been moving, slowly but surely, away from a concentration on constitutional rules and towards the more difficult but important concept of a realistic political education or the enhancement of political literacy.

This approach has, of course, been common enough in the universities for many years. Quite apart from its civic importance, the teaching of politics in schools has tended to lag behind university practice and expectations. So the editors have aimed to draw on the most up-to-date academic knowledge, the books being written by a wide spectrum of authors, but all aware of the need to combine accurate scholarship with lucid presentation.

The Politics Association and the editors are conscious of the great importance of other levels of education, and have been actively pursuing studies and projects of curriculum development in several directions. But A level and new developments in sixth-form courses are recognised as being important precisely because of the great overlap here between teaching in secondary school and further education colleges, whether specifically for examinations or not; indeed most of the books will be equally useful for general studies, just as several are also widely used by first year students in universities and polytechnics.

*Bernard Crick*
*Derek Heater*

# Preface

It was with some reluctance because of existing heavy commitments that I accepted the invitation of Bernard Crick and Derek Heater to write this book. The experience of writing it, however, has not only been useful, but enjoyable, and I am therefore grateful that I allowed myself to be persuaded. The book owes much to the many writers, past and present, who have written about British politics and, in particular, about the Cabinet and the Prime Minister; some of the views they have expressed have inevitably and properly found their way into the text. Apart from specific acknowledgements in the notes and references at the end of the book, a more general acknowledgement is made by listing many of the works concerned in the Select Bibliography. However, I take responsibility for the presentation of any opinions in the book, especially those in the final chapter on the controversy over prime ministerial government, and, of course, for any errors that may have occurred. Finally, a debt is owed to my wife, Jean, who not only encouraged me to accept the invitation to write this book but who continued to encourage me during its writing.

March 1982

*Michael Rush,*
*University of Exeter*

# 1 The British System of Government

The British system of government has been variously described as 'parliamentary government', 'cabinet government' and, more recently and controversially, as 'prime ministerial government'. In *constitutional* terms the most accurate of these descriptions is 'parliamentary government', which may be defined as that form of government in which the executive is drawn from and is constitutionally responsible to the legislature. Thus, with extremely limited and mostly temporary exceptions, the members of the Government from the most junior to the Prime Minister are also members of one of the two Houses of Parliament. The leading members of the Government constitute the Cabinet, which meets regularly and which, it is asserted, determines Government policy, hence the term 'cabinet government'. Whether the Cabinet does determine Government policy is a matter of dispute and another school of thought argues that it is really the Prime Minister who is the policy-maker, hence the term 'prime ministerial government'. The accuracy of these terms is a matter for later discussion.

The constitutional responsibility of the executive to the legislature means two things: first, that the Government must secure the confidence and retain the support of a majority in Parliament and, second, that ministers are collectively and individually answerable to Parliament for their conduct of affairs. In practice, 'Parliament' means the House of Commons and it is therefore from the House of Commons that the majority of ministers, including most of the Cabinet, are drawn and to the House of Commons that they are answerable. Once formed, the Government remains in office as long as it retains the support of a majority of MPs. The Government's legislative proposals become law only after they have been approved by both Houses of Parliament and the Government's policies and actions are the legitimate objects of parliamentary scrutiny.

Ministerial responsibility means that ministers and not civil servants are held constitutionally responsible for the conduct of affairs. Collective ministerial responsibility stipulates that, once made, Government decisions are binding on all ministers, regardless of whether they were directly involved in the making of such decisions. Any minister, junior or senior, who is not prepared to accept a Government decision is expected to resign and failure to do so may result in his dismissal. Individual ministerial responsibility means that ministers are accountable to Parliament for the running of their departments and for the conduct of civil servants in carrying out their departmental responsibilities. In short, save only for the reprehensible action of a civil servant, such as disobeying or failing to carry out an instruction, the civil servant's error is the minister's error. If Parliament feels that the minister has failed in his constitutional responsibility it can demand his resignation and, although it cannot constitutionally enforce his resignation, it can bring him under such pressure that he may feel constrained to resign.

Such is the constitutional situation, but the British constitution aptly illustrates Bismarck's dictum that 'politics is not an exact science'. The absence of a written constitution and the consequent reliance on a mass of constitutional practices obviously complicates the situation. These constitutional practices or *conventions* are an essential part of the system, consisting of rules of political practice which are generally accepted by politicians, but which would not be upheld by the courts in the event of an alleged failure to adhere to them. The constitutional role of the monarch, for example, is the product of constitutional conventions: government is carried on in the name of the Queen, but by convention in political matters the Queen acts entirely on the advice of her ministers. The situation is further complicated by the habit of deviating from some of these practices whilst continuing either to observe them in part or, in some cases, to pay no more than lip-service.

In the case of collective responsibility, for instance, in practice it is sometimes difficult to distinguish the application of the constitutional doctrine from straightforward political solidarity, in which collective responsibility is used as a means of hiding divisions within the ranks of the Government. Under these circumstances collective responsibility becomes a weapon in the hands of the Prime Minister for stifling criticism, discouraging morale-sapping dissension and avoiding politically damaging resignations. On a few occasions this century, however, the doctrine of collective responsibility has been suspended because it suited the Government of the day – something which is possible because the doctrine has no force in law. In 1912 it was suspended in relation to proposals for female suffrage; in 1931–2 over free trade; in 1975 over the referendum on Britain's membership of the EEC and in 1978 over legislation establishing direct elections to the European Parliament. Nonetheless, from time to time ministers do resign in accordance with the doctrine of collective responsibility because they are unwilling to accept one or more Government policies. Such resignations are relatively common, since resignation on the grounds of disagreement with Government policy is not necessarily damaging to a politician's career and a number have again achieved office after such resignations.

Resignations on the grounds of individual ministerial responsibility, however, are extremely rare – between Sir Thomas Dugdale in 1954 and Lord Carrington in 1982 there were no clear-cut cases. There are two basic reasons for this, the first being, quite properly, that resignation is the ultimate, not the only, punishment for ministerial failure. In some cases, of course, the failure may be that of civil servants rather than the minister and appropriate corrective action may be taken in the minister's department, although the minister still accepts public responsibility for any such failure. In other cases a reprimand from the Prime Minister may the most appropiate course of action, but not infrequently the second basic reason intervenes. This is, as in the case of collective responsibility, the strong tendency in British politics towards political solidarity. Other punishments exist between those of the reprimand and resignation, but they are generally used in a manner that does not link them overtly with the ministerial failure concerned. Thus, an offending minister may be denied promotion in a later reshuffle of ministerial posts, or quietly retired.

Parliamentary government is probably seen at its most mythical, however, when ministers solemnly state that the decision on this policy or that is, 'of course, a matter for Parliament to decide'. It is largely a myth because it omits all mention of a *party*. In spite of the fact that a knowledge of the party system is vital to an understanding of the operation of British politics – and has been since at least the late eighteenth century – statutory references to political parties are rare. It is a measure of its rarity that possibly the earliest reference was in 1937 when, in order to authorise the payment of a salary to the Leader of the Opposition, it was necessary to define him in the Ministers of the Crown Act as, 'that member of the House of Commons who is for the time being the Leader in that House of the *party* in opposition to His Majesty's Government having the greatest numerical strength in that House' (author's italics). Of greater irony, perhaps, is that fact that until 1969 the designation of a candidate's party on the ballot paper in elections was expressly forbidden and in order to vote for a particular party (as indicated by research into the electoral behaviour of voters), the voter had to remember which candidate was standing for the party of his choice. Even *Hansard*, the official record of parliamentary debates, does not record the party affiliation of MPs: the Member is simply recorded by name and the constituency represented, Division lists – which are invariably the product of differing party views – record only the names of the 'Ayes' and the 'Noes'.

There are occasions when a party fails to dominate the operation of Parliament, but these are the exceptions that prove the general rule. Private Members' Bills – that is, Bills promoted by backbench MPs rather than the Government, for example – are not subject to the party whips or instructions in the form of 'requests' as to how MPs should vote in various divisions. Any conflict on party lines over such Bills is not a consequence of the system of party discipline which largely determines the outcome of other divisions. However, only a handful of Private Members' Bills are passed each year, most failing through lack of time, since the greater part of parliamentary time is controlled by either the Government or the official Opposition. It is also true that from time to time the party whips are not imposed and a free vote is allowed, but this merely illustrates the primacy of party, since not only are free votes infrequent but the decision to allow such a vote is a *party* one. Finally, but no less important, there are occasions when one or more of the parties is divided over an issue and splits occur in spite of the imposition of the whip, but these too are relatively infrequent and again demonstrate the norm of party domination.

In terms of candidates nominated for election to Parliament, in electoral support, in MPs elected to the House of Commons and in the formation of Governments, political parties dominate British politics. Moreover, since 1868 that domination has, for the most part, been shared between two major parties: initially between Conservatives and Liberals and later between the Conservative and Labour Parties. In short, Britain has a two-party system rather than the multi-party systems found in some other countries. It is also the case that electoral support is fairly evenly divided between the two major parties, so that both have a reasonable expectation and experience of winning elections and holding office. This gives them a strong incentive to maintain the basic system of British government, since it is through that system that they secure political power. It is therefore not surprising that, in addition to the descriptions mentioned earlier, parliamentary government should also sometimes be described as 'party government'.

This description is given added force by virtue of the fact that for the greater part of the period since 1868 Britain has had Governments formed by a single party with a majority of MPs in the House of Commons. Minority Governments have occurred from time to time, most recently between February and October 1974 and from 1976 to 1979. Coalition Governments have been formed in times of great crisis, such as the two world wars and the economic crisis of 1931, but the norm is a single-party, majority Government. It is, however, not party government in the sense that it is the party which governs. Despite being drawn exclusively from the party, which undoubtedly exerts a significant influence, it is the Government that dominates the party rather than the reverse.

Two-party domination is further reinforced by the fact that not only do the leaders of the majority party form the Government of the day, but the leaders of the second largest party normally constitute the official Opposition. The Opposition organises and presents itself as an alternative to the Government, ready to assume office the moment the Government loses the confidence of the House of Commons (a rare occurrence in reality, in spite of the fall of the Callaghan administration in 1979) or loses its majority at a general election (the most common means by which one party replaces the other in office). The roles of Government and Opposition are institutionalised in Parliament in general, and in the House of Commons in particular, and the operation of Parliament rests almost entirely on this dichotomy. The allocation of parliamentary time and the setting of the parliamentary agenda are substantially in the hands or the Government and the Opposition, whilst debates reflect the dichotomy not only in the confrontation of Government and Opposition but in the physical layout of both Houses of Parliament, in which the Government occupies the benches to the right of Speaker and the Opposition those to the left. Furthermore, the day-to-day operation of Parliament depends heavily on cooperation between the Government and the Opposition through what are euphemistically known as 'the usual channels' – the Government's business manager, the Leader of the House, and his opposite number on the Opposition benches and the respective party whips. Even though the Government invariably has a majority, it needs the cooperation of the Opposition to secure the passage of its business, since the Opposition has available to it a number of procedural devices whose skilled and determined use can wreak havoc with the Government's programme. At the same time the Opposition has a strong incentive to cooperate most of the time, since it hopes and believes it will be in power after the next election at the very latest, when the roles of Government and Opposition would be reversed.

The Government in general, and the Cabinet in particular, therefore operate in the context of a party system which both reflects and shapes the parliamentary system. To analyse the role of the Cabinet in a solely constitutional context, on the one hand, or in the context of the party system on the other, is to ignore political reality.

# 2 The Development of the Cabinet

Dictionaries sometimes give words and phrases a certainty of meaning that is at best illusory, at worst misleading. Moreover, such meanings are often invested with a degree of permanence that distorts their historical usage. The political usage of the word 'cabinet' is a case in point. The term 'cabinet council', meaning a small group of political advisers to the monarch, can be traced back to at least the reign of James I (1603–25) in Francis Bacon's writings, and was certainly used in the reign of Charles I (1625–49). It was more commonly used, however, under Charles II (1660–85), but more often than not, both then and earlier, it was largely as a term of suspicion, criticism and abuse. The 'Cabinet Council' was, in fact, one of a number of terms employed during Charles II's reign for his immediate advisers, including the 'Cabinet', the 'Foreign Committee', the 'Committee of Intelligence', the 'Foreign Affairs Committee' and, most famous of all, the 'Cabal'. This latter term was also used under James I to describe his secret advisers, but achieved its greatest fame when the initials of Charles II's five ministers – Clifford, Arlington, Buckingham, Ashley and Lauderdale – happened by coincidence to spell the word 'cabal'.

It is an oversimplification, however, to see the Cabinet solely as the modern successor to the monarch's need for a group of political advisers. Monarchs certainly needed advisers, but historically they took a variety of forms, ranging from one or more trusted individuals (who might or might not hold some office of state) to institutional bodies of varying size.

Certainly various offices and bodies came to be established, but their functions and usage varied from one reign and period to another. Most kings found themselves in conflict with some of their more powerful subjects from time to time and some, such as John, Henry III and Edward II, had severe institutional and other constraints imposed upon them. Thus, existing offices and bodies often remained the same in name but varied in their importance, whilst on other occasions new offices and bodies were created, often for administrative and judicial purposes, and also as a means of securing influence and control over royal decisions and policies. This situation is further confused because the central role of the monarch in the governmental process meant that the distinction between the royal household and the governmental machine was inevitably blurred. Although this is no longer the case, a vestige of this blurring remains in the appointment of a number of Government whips in both Houses of Parliament as members of the royal household, such as the Comptroller of the Household, the Vice-Chamberlain of the Household, the Captain of the Gentlemen-at-Arms and the Captain of the Queen's Bodyguard. It is important to realise that although British constitutional history is characterised by continuity, it is a haphazard continuity and constitutional developments were invariably pragmatic responses to particular needs and situations, rather than the product of some holistic theory.

As far back as Saxon times the King sought and was expected to seek advice from the *witanagemot*, which consisted of the most powerful landowners and church leaders. One of the tasks of the *witan* was to elect a new king when necessary; on at least two occasions the *witan* actually deposed kings for misgovernment. It was only later, at the beginning of the fourteenth century, that the hereditary succession to the Crown was clearly established. Even so, Parliament subsequently claimed the right to depose the sovereign and designate a successor. Similarly, Norman and mediaeval kings ruled with the assistance of a council, comprising various officers of state and members of the royal household, leading judges, members of the clergy and of the aristocracy, and a number of specially appointed counsellors. The council was a fairly large body and kings invariably took advice from a small, inner group. Terms such as 'secret council' and 'private council' occur in governmental documents as early as the reign of Edward II (1307–27) and a recurrent theme in the development of the executive arm of government is the attempt by monarchs to create small advisory or decision-making bodies or groups, which would supersede larger bodies such as the council.

A parallel theme was the periodic tendency for these smaller bodies to become larger, thus building up pressure for the creation of another smaller, inner body. The development of the Privy Council – from which the modern Cabinet developed – illustrates both these themes. Historically the governmental process was clearly involved with the administration of justice and, although separate machinery for this purpose was gradually evolved, the link between the judicial process on the one hand and the political decision-making and administrative processes on the other has never been totally severed, as the role of the House of Lords as the final court of appeal in all civil and criminal cases illustrates.

The establishment of the Privy Council was partly a recognition of the need for a greater separation in the performance of these functions and partly a response to the need for a small advisory body drawn from the larger council. By the middle of the sixteenth century it had, under the Tudor monarchs, become firmly established at the centre of the political executive. In time, however, the Privy Council grew in size and became somewhat unwieldy, leading Charles II to argue that it was an inappropriate body for the confidential discussion of policy and the expeditious making of decisions. Charles II, in fact, had an ulterior motive in that he wished to exclude some members of the Privy Council from any knowledge of the policies he wished to pursue. He therefore resorted to using a small number of trusted Privy Councillors in the form of a committee, although in practice it did not always perform the true function of a committee since it did not necessarily report back to its parent body. However, it is because it remains constitutionally a committee of the Privy Council that the modern Cabinet can trace its origins back to at least the end of the seventeenth century. All members of the Privy Council are made Privy Councillors and the Cabinet is, in terms of offering advice to the sovereign, the active membership of the Privy Council. All other members of the Council, such as former Cabinet ministers, – whether members of the governing party or the Opposition – are excluded from active participation. Apart from on the accession of a new sovereign, the full Privy Council has not met since 1839 on the announcement of Queen Victoria's forthcoming marriage.

Nonetheless, the Privy Council does have important judicial and constitutional functions to perform. Its judicial functions consist of hearing appeals from various tribunals, British colonies and a few Commonwealth countries, and are carried out by the Judicial Committee of the Privy Council. The members of the Judicial Committee are drawn from senior members of the British judiciary and, where appropriate, from Commonwealth countries from which appeals lie. Its constitutional functions consist of giving legal effect to various decisions in the form of Proclamations or Orders-in-Council, and are carried out by those members of the Cabinet responsible for the matters concerned. The quorum for such purposes is only three members.

It would be an oversimplification to assume that the modern Cabinet dates from the time of the later Stuarts: it is one thing to trace it *origins*, but it is entirely another to trace its *establishment* from that period. The modern Cabinet is a product not of the end of the seventeenth century but of what has occurred since that time. Moreover, the course of history is such that there is nothing inevitable about the development of the Cabinet, and its present form owes much to the accidents of history.

One of the most important and well-known of these is the Hanoverian succession, which, in the persons of George I (1714–27) and George II (1727–60), produced monarchs whose relative lack of interest in English affairs was such that the politicians (in the persons of the King's ministers) came to play an even more prominent part in political affairs than they had under the later Stuarts. It was ironical, therefore, that when George III (1760–1820) sought to reassert royal influence at the beginning of his reign, his actions were denounced by his opponents as unconstitutional. In all probability the Hanoverian succession did no more than accelerate the process by which political power was passing from the monarch to the politicians. However, such observations are made with the benefit of hindsight and it is an assumption that the process was inevitable.

A better but less well-known example of a development which might have had a profound affect on the Cabinet and, indeed, on the whole political system, is the provision in the Act of Settlement, 1701 which stipulated that various office-holders, including ministers, were excluded from membership of the House of Commons. This provision was subsequently modified and ultimately repealed, but had it been enforced it would have created a partial separation of powers, similar to but less extensive than that which constitutes a major feature of the American political system. The United States Constitution expressly forbids the holders of executive office (the President and members of his Cabinet) to be members of the legislature – Congress. In the British case ministers could still have been drawn from the House of Lords, but not from the Commons and its purpose was to limit the ability of the Crown and ministers to influence and control the decisions of the lower house, which by this time had become constitutionally the more important of the two Houses of Parliament. Whether this provision would eventually have led to a total separation of powers on American lines is a matter for speculation, but even the exclusion of ministers from the Commons would almost certainly have radically altered the subsequent development of the political system, and therefore of the the the Cabinet. In particular, it is highly unlikely that a Cabinet constitutionally responsible to the legislature would have developed.

Attention is thus directed to the vitally important fact that at the time of the Act of Settlement (and until at least well into the nineteenth century) the unequivocal constitutional responsibility of the Government of the day to Parliament in general, and the House of Commons in particular, was far from established. In fact, for most of the eighteenth century the confidence of the monarch was more important than that of the House of Commons, and Governments could and did survive in spite of hostile majorities in the Commons. By the Reform Act of 1832, however, it was acknowledged that no Government could survive without the confidence of the House of Commons, but as late as 1839 Sir Robert Peel declined to form a Government on the grounds that he did not have the confidence of the Queen.

The Reform Act of 1832 also provides a further important watershed: in the eighteenth century the Government could rely on winning any election through the prevailing system of bribery, corruption and influence. Prior to 1832 Governments fell not because they lost elections, but because they had lost royal confidence (especially in the eighteenth century) or because they were *unwilling* to continue without majority support in the House of Commons. After 1832 Governments occasionally fell through a failure to maintain majority support in the House, especially between 1846 and 1868, when the modern party system was emerging. After 1832, however, Governments also lost office by being beaten at general elections, although the full impact of this was not realised until after 1867, when a substantial extension of the franchise necessitated the general creation of party organisation outside Parliament to contest elections.

Other developments occurred during the eighteenth and nineteenth centuries which were even more pertinent to the growth of the modern Cabinet. The most significant of these were the development of the office of Prime Minister, of the Cabinet as a coherent body of ministers, and of the doctrine of ministerial responsibility.

The term 'Prime Minister' was often used pejoratively as were the terms 'Cabinet' and 'Cabal'. Historically Sir Robert Walpole is widely regarded as the 'first Prime Minister' and his portrait hangs as such in No 10 Downing Street. It was, however, one of the major criticisms of Walpole immediately before his fall from office in 1742 that he was 'Prime Minister' and his opponents argued that the constitution did not recognise such an office or person. They argued instead, that each minister had responsibility for a particular department and should exercise that responsibility without interference from other ministers. This is not to say that they were arguing that some form of Cabinet government existed or ought to exist, since there is little doubt that whilst consultation between ministers in the form of periodic but irregular 'Cabinet meetings' occurred, the Cabinet was not a coherent and regular decision-making body. Moreover, it is important to remember that ministers were constitutionally responsible to the King rather than to Parliament for the running of their departments, and the King could and did consult individual ministers.

There can be little doubt that Walpole dominated his fellow-ministers, but he did this by virtue of his political skills and the strength of his personality, not because of the office he held. Like Walpole, modern Prime Ministers hold the office of First Lord of the Treasury, but few of Walpole's successors as First Lord achieved his degree of dominance. Indeed, one of the most dominant figures later in the eighteenth century. William Pitt the Elder (later the Earl of Chatham), did not hold the office of First Lord. Nor was Walpole the last of the King's ministers to be attacked on the grounds that he was 'Prime Minister': forty years after Walpole denied being Prime Minister, so did Lord North. By 1803, however, William Pitt the Younger confidently asserted that the position of Prime Minister was a necessary part of the political system and it was Pitt himself who had done much to bring this about. His dominance of the Cabinet and his astute management of both King and the House of Commons were such that what had been a term applied to the dominant personality in each Government, often as a form of abuse, had now become an *office*. It remained a title recognised only by convention until it was mentioned first in the ceremonial order of precedence earlier this century and then in the Ministers of the Crown Act, 1937.

The establishment of the office of Prime Minister could not have been achieved, however, without the precedents of ministers like Walpole and the Elder Pitt, and the gradual recognition that neither 'government by departments' nor some form of 'collective leadership' of the Cabinet were adequate substitutes for a clearly-designated leader of the Government; a role performed by the monarch in earlier times.

Just as it is possible to push back the existence of the office of Prime Minister further than a strict interpretation of the historical facts will bear, the Cabinet can also be treated in a similar fashion. That the Cabinet existed in the eighteenth century cannot be denied, but it differed in a number of important respects from its modern counterpart. Apart from the fact that it sometimes lacked a clearly designated leader in the person of the Prime Minister, the eighteenth-century Cabinet was not based upon a clearly defined party system in the modern sense of the term. This was not simply because the Whigs and Tories lacked the extensive extra-parliamentary organisations that are so much a part of modern political parties, but more fundamentally because they were much looser associations of like-minded men who did not dominate Parliament *numerically* in the same way as the later Conservatives and Liberals, or the modern Conservative and Labour Parties. Their power rested not on the firm basis of an elected party majority, but on their ability to secure and retain the support of significant proportions of MPs who did not acknowledge a continuing allegiance to either Whigs or Tories. In fact, both Whigs and Tories were split into various factions; as the eighteenth century progressed it was not uncommon to find Cabinets consisting of both Whig and Tory politicians. Moreover, like 'Cabinet' and 'Prime Minister', the term 'party' was often one of abuse and regarded as synonymous with faction. Those MPs who acknowledged no continuing allegiance were open to persuasion, but more particularly to the fruits of patronage, bribery and corruption. It has been cynically observed, however, that many were more than willing to accept an inducement to vote the way they had already decided to vote.

This system was undermined to some extent by limited reforms in the latter part of the eighteenth century, which reduced the Government's ability to dispense patronage and largesse to its supporters and to the limited number of voters in elections, but the system finally broke down with the extension of the franchise, beginning in 1832 and followed by further major extensions in 1867 and 1884. Once the politicians had to win the support of a large electorate, it became necessary for them to form electoral organisations outside Parliament and to present to the electorate a programme of policies which, they hoped, would win its support. The organisational vehicle for this process was the modern political party.

The advent of the modern political party reinforced the already existing tendency for the Cabinet to operate as a coherent body, headed by a clearly designated Prime Minister. In the middle of the eighteenth century it was by no means unusual for Cabinet ministers to speak against Government proposals in Parliament and as late as 1783 a member of the Cabinet spoke against Fox's India Bill in the House of Lords. Furthermore, it was common during the eighteenth century for particular members of the Cabinet to continue in office when the First Lord of the Treasury resigned, in direct contrast to the modern practice of all ministers leaving office when the Prime Minister resigns. Pitt the Younger was the first Prime Minister clearly to establish the Prime Minister's right to insist on the resignation of a minister, and nineteenth-century Cabinets increasingly followed the modern pattern of coherence.

This coherence manifested itself particularly in the development of ministerial responsibility. Once it was accepted that the existence of the Government depended upon its securing and retaining the confidence of the House of Commons, it was understandable that the constitutional responsibility of the executive to the legislature should become a major feature of parliamentary government. The convention of collective responsibility was reinforced in practice by the obvious advantages of political solidarity, with the Government maintaining a united front against all opposition, whilst the convention of individual ministerial responsibility was reinforced by the growing interest that Parliament showed in governmental policies during the nineteenth century.

By the time of Gladstone and Disraeli the foundations of the modern political system had been firmly laid and a noted observer of the period, Walter Bagehot, in *The English Constitution* (first published in 1867) was able to describe the Cabinet as the crucial institution of Government. Bagehot focused attention on the vital institutional relationship between the executive, in the form of the Cabinet, and the legislature, in the form of Parliament. He argued that this relationship made the Cabinet the 'efficient secret' of the constitution. What he meant by this was that government was still carried on in the name of the monarch – a role to which he assigned the term 'dignified' – but that in reality it was the Cabinet that made political decisions. He described its role as 'secret' because of the monarchical facade behind which it operated, and 'efficient' because having the support of a majority in the House of Commons, it could provide firm and effective government and yet remain sensitive to criticism through its constitutional responsibility to Parliament.

Bagehot was writing just as the modern party system was beginning to emerge, however, and he did not fully anticipate the strong, disciplined parties that would come to dominate the political system. In particular he did not envisage a situation in which the Government controlled the House of Commons through its party majority, rather than the Commons controlling the Government in the sense of having a significant influence over policy and, ultimately, the ability to make or break Governments. More recent writers – notably the late Richard Crossman, a prominent Labour politician and former Cabinet Minister – have argued that Bagehot's 'efficient secret' has passed from the Cabinet to the

Prime Minister. Even assuming that this is an accurate assessment of the contemporary situation, there is no doubt that Bagehot was right to focus attention on the Cabinet for, whether or not it is now dominated by the Prime Minister, it remains at the centre of the governmental machine.

There has been one other important change since Bagehot's day and that is the enormous expansion in the size of the governmental machine. This is largely the result of the vast expansion in governmental activities due partly to changing ideological views on the desirability and efficacy of governmental intervention in the affairs of society, and partly to public demand that Governments should provide solutions to an increasingly wide range of problems. Understandably, both changing ideological views and public demand have tended to feed each other, whilst the need to win elections has encouraged politicians and parties to claim that they have the policies which will solve society's problems. The implication of these developments for the Cabinet is that it now stands at the head of a ministerial hierarchy which is constitutionally responsible for the running of a complex administrative machine, in the form of the Civil Service. This has produced an expansion in the size of the Cabinet, but an even greater expansion in the size of the Government as a whole.

In the eighteenth century the Cabinet and the Ministry or Government were more or less synonymous; only the holders of a few unimportant offices were excluded from the Cabinet. During the nineteenth century, however, the number of posts outside the Cabinet gradually increased, until by 1900 there were no less than sixty ministerial appointments, including nineteen members of the Cabinet. The Cabinet expanded from five or six in the middle of the eighteenth century to thirteen or fourteen in the middle of the nineteenth and now usually consists of more than twenty ministers, whilst the total number of ministerial posts now usually exceeds a hundred. These posts are at the disposal of the Prime Minister, but in filling them the Prime Minister must take a number of factors into account, especially when appointing Cabinet ministers: politics has been called the art of the possible, and nowhere is this more true than in recruiting or forming the Cabinet.

# 3 Making a Cabinet

Harold Macmillian once boasted, tongue in cheek, that his Cabinet was superior to Attlee's because it contained more Old Etonians! In socio-economic terms the Cabinet is, and always has been, a largely elitist body in the sense that its members tend to be drawn from the higher echelons of society, whether the latter are defined in terms of educational and occupational criteria, or more loosely in terms of family background and status. In this respect, however, the Cabinet differs only in degree from the Government as a whole and from the House of Commons.

There are socio-economic differences between Conservative and Labour MPs, with a much higher proportion of Conservatives coming from public schools and 'Oxbridge' backgrounds and, not surprisingly, a substantial proportion with business backgrounds. Labour, on the other hand, is better represented amongst the professions and those with manual occupations. Nonetheless, the majority of MPs in both major parties would, by objective criteria, be described as middle class, with Conservatives being drawn largely from the upper, and Labour MPs from the lower echelons of that class. Indeed, although less than one-fifth of Labour MPs have attended public schools or are 'Oxbridge' graduates, the proportions are still substantially higher than for the population in general. Similarly, more than half of all Labour MPs are now university graduates – a much higher proportion than the national average. This has not always been so; until 1922 Labour MPs were, again by objective criteria, almost entirely working class in background. Since 1922, however, the Labour Party's representatives at Westminster have become increasingly middle class in background, although many Labour MPs can, and do, claim working class antecedents.

A great deal is often made of the elitist nature of the House of

17

Commons, which is inevitably reflected in the composition of the Government and the Cabinet, but there is no evidence that it plays an overt part in the actual selection of ministers. From the point of view of elite theorists and Marxists great significance is attached to the socio-economic backgrounds of those who secure political office. Furthermore, even without subscribing to either elite or Marxist theory, it is possible that Governments would behave differently if their members came from backgrounds which were substantially different from those of contemporary politicians. This is a matter of speculation, however, and only limited results have been produced by empirical research investigating the existence of a causal relationship between socio-economic background and political behaviour. It is also argued that legislative bodies and political office holders should be socio-economically representatives of the population at large. This too is a matter of speculation and this chapter is primarily concerned with the circumstances and factors which are undoubtedly taken into account when the Prime Minister forms a Cabinet.

It is important to bear in mind that the Cabinet is at the top of a complex ministerial hierarchy and much that applies to the recruitment of the Cabinet also applies to the recruitment of the Government as a whole. The situation is complicated by the fact that the Prime Minister may, within certain limits, vary the composition of the Cabinet, being true both of its size and the ministerial offices it encompasses, as well as of its personnel. In practice, no one Cabinet differs markedly from another in size or in ministerial offices, although important variations can occur, especially when the Prime Minister seeks to create a smaller than usual Cabinet. Broadly speaking, however, the twenty or so most senior ministers constitute the Cabinet. Most of these ministers will be in charge of a particular department, such as the Treasury, the Foreign and Commonwealth Office, the Home Office, the Department of Health and Social Security or the Scottish Office. Apart from the Chancellor of the Exchequer, who heads the Treasury, and the Ministers of Agriculture and Transport, departmental heads have the title Secretary of State, although it is common to refer in some cases to the Foreign Secretary or the Home Secretary.

Apart from the departmental heads a small number of ministers hold sinecure posts, ie, positions with only limited responsibilities directly related to the office concerned. These ministers are given specific responsibilities which vary from one administration to another. In the Cabinet formed by Margaret Thatcher in May 1979, for example, Lord Soames (the Government Leader or business manager in the House of Lords),was made Lord President of the Council, and was also made responsible for Civil Service affairs. The Foreign Office spokesman in the House of Commons, Sir Ian Gilmour, was appointed Lord Privy Seal. This appointment was necessary because the Foreign Secretary, Lord Carrington, was a member of the House of Lords. The Leader of the House of Commons (the Government's business manager in that house) Norman St John Stevas, became Chancellor of the Duchy of Lancaster. Finally, Angus Maude, who was placed in charge of government information services and public relations, was given the post of Paymaster-General.

Until relatively recently it was the practice of Prime Ministers to exclude some departmental heads from membership of the Cabinet, but with the tendency to amalgamate departments which occurred in the 1960s and 1970s, almost all departmental heads are now members of the Cabinet. At various times during the Wilson administration of 1964–70, however, the Minister of Overseas Development was not a member of the Cabinet, and in May 1979 Margaret Thatcher excluded the Minister of Transport from her Cabinet.

In addition to any senior ministers outside the Cabinet there are four Law Officers – the Attorney-General, his deputy the Solicitor-General, the Lord Advocate, and his deputy, the Solicitor-General for Scotland. These last two posts are necessary because Scotland has its own legal system. The Law Officers, together with the Lord Chancellor (who is a member of the Cabinet and head of the judiciary) are responsible for administering the two legal systems of the United Kingdom and for advising the Government on the legal aspects and implications of its policies.

Each Government department has one or more middle rank and junior ministers. Middle rank ministers have the title of Minister of State and junior ministers of Parliamentary Secretary (or Parliamentary Under-Secretary where the departmental head is a Secretary of State). The responsibilities of most departments are divided amongst the middle rank and junior ministers and in some cases Ministers of State are commonly referred to as Minister of Health, or Minister for Sport, although they are not in fact departmental heads.

Finally, in both Houses of Parliament the routine management of the Government's business is in the hands of the two Government chief whips and their subordinates. The whips are, in a sense, the epitome of the close relationship that exists between the Government and the legislature: they are the Government's eyes and ears in Parliament, as well as being the messengers of its will.

These appointments constitute the members of the Government, but there is, below this governmental hierarchy, a further group of appointees. These are Parliamentary Private Secretaries (PPS), who are unpaid, personal aides to ministers. They have no official status, but usually act as liaison officers between the minister and the Government's backbench supporters, and are expected to observe the convention of collective ministerial responsibility. The position of a PPS is widely seen as the first step towards ministerial office, although the appointment of a PPS is made by the minister concerned and not by the Prime Minister. Nonetheless, the Prime Minister can insist on the dismissal of a PPS in the event of failure to observe collective responsibility.

Table 3.1: *The Composition of the Government, May 1979*

| Rank | Number |
|---|---|
| Cabinet | 22 |
| Senior non-Cabinet | 1 |
| Law Officer | 4 |
| Minister of State | 27 |
| Parliamentary Secretary | 31 |
| Whip | 15 |
| *Total* | 100 |

The distribution of ministers amongst the various levels of the hierarchy varies from one Government to another, depending very much on the views of the Prime Minister concerned. For instance, the Government formed by Margaret Thatcher has a larger proportion of Ministers of State than any previous Government, but the number of senior non-Cabinet ministers has been reduced to one. The size of the Cabinet can also vary: the largest ever being that formed by James Callaghan following a Cabinet reconstruction necessitated by the death of Anthony Crosland in February 1977; and the smallest peace-time Cabinet this century being that formed by Winston Churchill in 1951, which had sixteen members. Nonetheless, the variations in size are not great because in practice the Prime Minister has only limited room for manoeuvre.

What factors therefore influence a Prime Minister in forming a Government in general, and the Cabinet in particular? The constraints are such that, although the formation of most Governments produces some surprises, it is not difficult to make generalisations about ministerial recruitment. Moreover, the surprises that do occur are invariably exceptions that prove the general rule of the constraints, which are partly constitutional, but mainly and, not surprisingly, political.

The principal constitutional constraints relate to the relationship between the executive and the legislature. On the one hand there is a well-established convention that all ministers must normally be members of either the House of Lords or the House of Commons and, on the other, there is a statutory limitation on the number of MPs who may hold ministerial office. This latter constraint stems from the historic fear of Parliament that the Government could control or, at very least, substantially influence Parliament's deliberations and proceedings through the patronage of ministerial office. As was noted in Chapter 2, the Act of Settlement originally sought to prevent MPs from holding ministerial office and, although this provision was soon abandoned, the Prime Minister is prevented by the House of Commons Disqualification Act, 1975 from appointing more than ninety-five MPs to ministerial posts; a statutory restriction also exists on the number of ministers who may be appointed in each rank. However, such legislative restrictions can be eased (and have been on a number of occasions) by the simple device of passing amending legislation and do not, therefore, unduly restrict a Prime Minister's freedom of choice.

The constraints imposed by constitutional convention, however, are rather more important in practice. In the first place, it means that the Prime Minister will only rarely look outside Parliament for ministerial recruits. The only common exceptions to this rule are the appointments of the Scottish Law Officers, (the Lord Advocate and the Solicitor-General for Scotland) who must be members of the Scottish Bar – an insufficiently common qualification amongst MPs to guarantee suitable recruits. Other exceptions occur from time to time, but these almost invariably prove to be temporary since the individual concerned will either be made a member of the House of Lords by being made a life peer or – though not without difficulty – found a seat in the House of Commons through a by-election. In 1964, for example, Harold Wilson appointed Frank Cousins, then General Secretary of the Transport and General Workers' Union, Minister of Technology. Cousins was found a seat in the Commons through the creation of a by-election vacancy at Nuneaton; in 1979 Margaret Thatcher appointed Irwin Bellow, a Leeds City Councillor, a Parliamentary Secretary, and satisfied the convention by making him a life peer.

This convention arises because ministers are constitutionally responsible to Parliament, and that responsibility must in part be fulfilled by ensuring that ministers can promote and defend their policies *in* Parliament by participating directly in its proceedings. Unless there are very exceptional reasons (such as occurred in both world wars when leading Imperial or Commonwealth statesmen were made members of the War Cabinet) failure to satisfy the convention normally leads to resignation. This was the fate of Patrick Gordon Walker who became Foreign Secretary in the Labour Government formed as a result of the General Election of 1964 but who had the misfortune to be defeated in the election. As in the case of Frank Cousins, a by-election vacancy was created, but Gordon Walker was again defeated, resigned as Foreign Secretary, and did not hold office again until after his return to the Commons following the General Election of 1966.

This convention has further ramifications, however, concerning the distribution of offices between the two Houses of Parliament. Naturally, the Government needs spokesmen to conduct its business in both houses, but this is a matter of common sense rather than convention. With major exceptions of the Chancellor of the Exchequer (the Government's principal financial minister) on the one hand, and the Lord Chancellor, the Speaker of the House of Lords, on the other, the holders of most ministerial posts could have been in either house a hundred years ago. The Chancellor of the Exchequer was, and is, a member of the lower house because of the historic financial primacy of the Commons over the Lords. The Lord Chancellor was, and is, a member of the upper house because of his position as its Speaker and also because he is head of the judiciary, the House of Lords in its judicial capacity being the highest court of appeal. As recently as 1900 even the Prime Minister could be a member of the upper house, but, whilst serious consideration was given to the claims of Lord Curzon to be Prime Minister in 1923 and to those of Lord Halifax in 1940, none has been considered since. However, the special circumstances of 1963 resulting from the passing of the Peerages Act earlier that year, enabled Lord Home (Sir Alec Douglas-Home) and Lord Hailsham (Quintin Hogg) to disclaim their peerages and become rivals for the succession to Harold Macmillan.

That the Prime Minister must be a member of the House of Commons is now a clear convention and, following the disclaimer of his peerage and his election as Leader of the Conservative Party, it was incumbent upon Sir Alec Douglas-Home to seek and secure election to the Commons, which he did. How far this applies to other ministers is less clear. A widespread feeling exists, especially in the Labour Party, that the general primacy of the Commons demands that all ministers who are heads of Government departments should be MPs. However, it would, be somewhat premature to say that there is a clear convention to this effect, since there have been major exceptions in recent years, which means either that the convention (if such exists) has been breached, or that there is no convention. Thus in 1960 Lord Home (as he then was) became Foreign Secretary, in 1970 Lord Carrington became Secretary of State for Defence and, in 1979, became Foreign Secretary.

Since the exceptions all involve appointments made by Conservative Prime Ministers, it is safe to say that the Labour Party would like to see such a convention clearly accepted, whereas the

Conservative Party is not yet (if at all) ready to recognise its existence. Indeed, should the Labour Party implement its declared policy of abolishing the House of Lords the need for such a convention would be obviated. Nonetheless, with these occasional exceptions, departmental heads are now drawn from the House of Commons and the number of peers appointed to ministerial posts generally has declined markedly since the beginning of this century. In recent Governments the number has varied from fifteen and sixteen in the administrations of James Callaghan (1977) and Edward Heath (1970) respectively, to twenty in the Governments of Harold Wilson (1964) and Margaret Thatcher (1979).

As far as the Cabinet itself is concerned, the number of peers nowadays is very small. Harold Wilson's Cabinet of 1964, for example, included only two peers, which is in effect the minimum, since the Cabinet would normally include the Lord Chancellor and the Government Leader in the House of Lords, who normally holds a sinecure post, such as Lord Privy Seal or Lord President of the Council. Recent Conservative Cabinets hardly offered peers any greater representation, with both Edward Heath and Margaret Thatcher appointing only three peers to their Cabinets.

Parliament in general, and the House of Commons in particular, therefore provide the principal avenue to ministerial office and, more especially, to Cabinet office. It is more important than mere membership of Parliament, however, for, by the time they first become members of the Cabinet most ministers have served a lengthy parliamentary apprenticeship. Thus, the fifty-eight Labour ministers who were members of the Cabinet at various times between 1964 and 1970, and between 1974 and 1979 had, on first joining the Cabinet, an average length of parliamentary service of 14.8 years. The corresponding figure for the thirty-eight Conservatives who served in the Cabinet between 1970 and 1974 or who were first appointed to the Cabinet in 1979 was 13.2 years.

Furthermore, most politicians will not only have served a *parliamentary* apprenticeship prior to entry to the Cabinet, but a *ministerial* apprenticeship as well. Thus when a Prime Minister comes to form a new Government (usually after winning a General Election) the potential Cabinet ministers available will, in most cases, be able to offer a combination of extensive parliamentary and ministerial experience, including in some cases previous membership of the Cabinet, since the careers of many politicians span the lives of more than one Government formed by their party.

Table 3.2. *Parliamentary service and ministerial experience of Cabinet ministers in 1964, 1970, 1974 and 1979*

|  | | 1964 Wilson | 1970 Heath | 1974 Wilson | 1979 Thatcher |
|---|---|---|---|---|---|
| A. | Parliamentary service | *Years in Parliament** | | | |
|  | Mean | 16.7 | 19.0 | 21.7 | 19.3 |
|  | Median | 19 | 17 | 23 | 18 |
|  | Range | 0–28 | 9–35 | 10–29 | 9–41 |
| B. | Ministerial experience | % | % | % | % |
|  | Previous Cabinet office | 17.4 | 55.6 | 66.7 | 54.5 |
|  | Non-Cabinet office | 39.1 | 33.3 | 28.6 | 31.8 |
|  | None | 43.5 | 11.1 | 4.7 | 13.6 |
|  | *Totals* | 100.0 | 100.0 | 100.0 | 99.9 |
|  | Number of members of the Cabinet | 23 | 18 | 21 | 22 |

*\*Note*: Including membership of the House of Lords.

With the important exception of the Cabinet formed by Harold Wilson in 1964, the pattern of parliamentary service and ministerial experience shown in Table 3.2 is remarkably consistent. In 1964 the Labour Party was forming a Government for the first time for thirteen years and it is therefore not surprising that only four members of Wilson's Cabinet, including Wilson himself, had previously held Cabinet office. Even so, well over half had previously held ministerial office and, although the mean length of parliamentary service was 16.7 years, this rises to 18.3 years if Lord Gardiner and Frank Cousins (neither of whom had had any parliamentary experience prior to taking office) are excluded. In 1924, when the first Labour Government took office, even fewer members of the Cabinet had had ministerial experience, let alone the experience of Cabinet office; even the Prime Minister, Ramsay Macdonald, was having his first experience of office, although he had been an MP for fourteen years. In fact, Macdonald sought to strenthen his Government by recruiting individuals with ministerial experience from outside the Labour Party, notably from Liberals or former Liberals.

The fact that Parliament is the normal recruiting ground for the Cabinet means that those appointed are, almost without exception, career politicians who are experienced in both Parliament and ministerial office. Given the norm of single party majority Government, however, they are not only career politicians but party politicians and the Cabinet normally consists of the leading members of the Prime Minister's party. This places a further constraint on the Prime Minister's formation of the Cabinet – the needs of party. The Prime Minister must take into account the balance of forces within the party, both in terms of ideological and policy differences, and in terms of personalities. Some leading candidates for Cabinet office will be past or future contenders for the post of party leader and, therefore, actual or potential rivals of the Prime Minister; some are the acknowledged representatives of particular strands of opinion in the party or strongly identified with particular policies; some are powerful personalities or particularly able individuals, or both, whose presence will strengthen and give credibility to the Cabinet.

In both major parties individuals are identified as being on the left, the right, or at the centre of the ideological spectrum within the party. In addition, when a Government is formed following a period in Opposition, most of those appointed to the Cabinet will have served as Opposition frontbench spokesmen, usually as a member of the 'Shadow Cabinet'. Since the predispositions and personalities of the leading members of the party are well-known, at least in political circles, and since the Opposition organises and presents itself as an alternative Government, the membership of a newly-formed Cabinet is fairly predictable. This is true not only in respect of individual members, but also in the allocation of portfolios, which, to a significant degree, are allocated in accordance with the individuals' 'shadow' responsibilities. The political correspondents of the newspapers, radio and television will therefore have little difficulty in naming the majority of those who can expect Cabinet appointments, and not much more difficulty in matching names with offices.

Nevertheless, this does not prevent the Prime Minister from taking the pundits by surprise from time to time and making a totally unexpected appointment, either by bringing in someone from outside Parliament or by promoting someone straight from the backbenches. In 1964, for instance, Harold Wilson appointed two outsiders to his Cabinet – Gerald Gardiner and Frank Cousins. The appointment of Gerald Gardiner as Lord Chancellor and his consequent elevation to the peerage were not totally unexpected, but the appointment of Frank Cousins as Minister of Technology was a surprise. Clement Attlee also made some unexpected appointments in forming his first Cabinet in 1945, notably in making Aneurin Bevan Minister of Health, whilst Edward Heath caused some surprise when he made John Davies – a former Director-General of the Confederation of British Industries – Minister of Technology in 1970, although this last appointment came about initially because of the sudden death of Heath's Chancellor of the Exchequer, Iain Macleod, and the consequential ministerial changes.

The Prime Minister also needs to take account of the political and adminstrative skills required to fulfil the role of a Cabinet minister. All Cabinet posts to a greater or lesser degree involve exercising the mostly private (but sometimes public) skills of evolving and negotiating policies; the mostly public (but sometimes private) skills of presenting and defending policies; and of the largely private skills of implementing policies through administration. Most ministers are involved in policy discussions and negotiations with their fellow Cabinet members, and many are periodically involved in discussions and negotiations with various outside interests – such as trade unions and business organisations – and, especially since Britain became a member of the EEC, with the representatives of foreign Governments. Ministers are, of course, expected to present and defend their departments' policies in Parliament and, where appropriate, to take the administrative decisions necessary for the implementation of those policies.

The balance of skills required varies from one post to another, and over time. Some ministers, such as the Chancellor of the Exchequer, the Foreign Secretary or the Home Secretary, are bound to be frequently in the public eye because of the importance of the posts they hold; others may temporarily be the subject of much attention because of the importance the Government attaches to a particular policy, or because a particular issue has resulted in demands for Government action. Some departments, such as the Department of Health and Social Security, with its responsibility for the National Health Service and the provision of various welfare benefits and services – or the Department of the Environment, with its responsibility for housing and local government – involve their ministers in a good deal of administrative work. Other departments, such as the Foreign and Commonwealth Office or those offices related to the various sinecure posts, such as Lord President or Chancellor of the Duchy of Lancaster, are administratively less demanding. Each post requires a different mix of skills, and individual Governments have different policy priorities, all of which are likely to have an important effect on the Prime Minister's choice of Cabinet colleagues.

The whole problem is complicated, however, by the fact that the Prime Minister does not have a free choice in reality. Some leading members of the Prime Minister's party are far too important to be omitted from the Cabinet, and one or two are so important that they can be almost certain of receiving one of the key posts of Chancellor, Foreign Secretary or Home Secretary. Thus, the appointment as Cabinet ministers of Herbert Morrison and Ernest Bevin in 1945; Anthony Eden and R. A. Butler in 1951; George Brown and James Callaghan in 1964; Iain Macleod and Reginald Maudling in 1970; Michael Foot and Denis Healey in 1974; and, of Sir Geoffrey Howe and Sir Keith Joseph in 1979, were regarded as foregone conclusions, even if the post concerned was not in every case fully anticipated. As for the rest, their inclusion, if not always inevitable, is in most cases predictable, and the Prime Minister's principal task is to allocate the various posts. It is in allocating those posts, however, that the skills of Cabinet formation are most important; achieving a workable blend of ideological balance, policy priorities and political and administrative skills is of crucial importance to the future operation of the resultant Cabinet.

Once the Cabinet is formed the Prime Minister periodically has the opportunity to modify its membership through casual vacancies, or through more extensive ministerial reshuffles. Casual vacancies may be forced upon the Prime Minister by the death or resignation of a minister because of ill health or some other personal reason, or where a minister feels unable to accept Government policy and insists on resigning in protest. In such cases the Prime Minister may simply fill the vacancy by bringing in someone from outside the Cabinet or sometimes by limited changes within the Cabinet. On other occasions the Prime Minister may take the opportunity to effect more extensive ministerial changes involving not only the Cabinet but the whole Government. In either case the same criteria apply as in the original formation of the Cabinet, with the important exception that such changes provide an opportunity to bring new blood into the Cabinet. A Cabinet formed after a period in Opposition however, may be significantly affected by the need to reward those senior members of the party who have loyally supported it during its period out of power.

The extent to which *calculated* ministerial reshuffles occur varies from one Prime Minister to another. Between 1964 and 1970, for example, Harold Wilson had no less than six major reshuffles. Compared with this, Edward Heath had only two major reshuffles between 1970 and 1974. On average this meant that Wilson had a major reshuffle once a year, compared with once every two years for Heath. The arguments for and against periodic changes are not difficult to state: the introduction of new men and ideas may reinvigorate the Government and keep civil servants from being complacent, but a minister may no sooner become familiar with the operation of his department and the policies for which it is responsible, than he finds himself transferred to some other post with totally different responsibilites, whilst frequent changes may increase the possibility that civil servants will dominate ministers.

No ministerial reshuffle involves the whole of the Cabinet, however, and how long each minister remains a member of the Cabinet and how long each retains a particular post, is something that varies from individual to individual. Just under two-fifths of the twenty-three members of Harold Wilson's 1964 Cabinet, including the Prime Minister himself, were still members of the Cabinet in June 1970 when the Labour Government left office following its electoral defeat. In contrast, more than four-fifths of Edward Heath's original Cabinet of June 1970 were still in the Cabinet when the Conservatives left office in March 1974 following their electoral defeat. There is, of course, a difference in time scale, but even allowing for this the contrast remains.

Such figures can be somewhat misleading, however, since some ministers may hold a particular office for all or most of the Government's period of office, whilst others may have only a short tenure of a particular office. Three members of Wilson's 1964 Cabinet, for instance, held the same posts for the whole of the period 1964 to 1970. These were Lord Gardiner as Lord Chancellor, Denis Healey as Secretary of State for Defence and William Ross as Secretary of State for Scotland. More recently, Denis Healey was Chancellor of the Exchequer throughout the life of the 1974–9 Labour Government. Some indication of the extent to which ministerial tenure of office varies can be seen in Table 3.3.

Table 3.3. *Tenure of selected\* ministerial offices between 1900 and 1914 and between 1955 and 1970*

A.  Length of tenure

|         | Months in office | | |
|---------|------|--------|-----------|
|         | Mean | Median | Range     |
| 1900–14 | 34.4 | 33.0   | 27.5–82.5 |
| 1955–70 | 26.1 | 25.7   | 18.0–45.0 |

B.  Number of holders of office

|         | Mean | Median | Range |
|---------|------|--------|-------|
| 1900–14 | 4.8  | 5      | 2–6   |
| 1955–70 | 6.9  | 7      | 4–10  |

*Source*:  Richard Rose, 'The making of Cabinet ministers' in Valentine Herman and James E. Alt (eds.), *Cabinet Studies: A Reader*, Macmillan, 1975, p. 22.

*Note*:  The offices covered were the Foreign Office, Chancellor of the Exchequer, Home Secretary, Minister of Defence (calculated for the period 1900–14 by averaging the tenures of the First Lord of the Admiralty and the Minister of War), Minister of Housing and Local Government, Minister of Education, President of the Board of Trade, Secretary of State for Scotland, Minister of Agriculture, Postmaster-General and Minister of Public Buildings and Works.

Not all the offices used to calculate the figures in Table 3.3 were necessarily always in the Cabinet, since the exact departmental composition of the Cabinet is a matter for the Prime Minister. Nonetheless, these figures demonstrate that there is a considerable turnover in ministerial office and that between 1955 and 1970 each minister held a particular office for just over two years on average, and each department had an average of seven different ministers. Account should be taken however, of the average tenure of eighteen months for Education, to three and three quarter years for the Scottish Office. Table 3.3 also shows that, compared with the period 1900–14, the turnover in 1955–70 was noticeably greater and the tenure of office therefore shorter.

Such considerations have important implications for the operation of the Cabinet, since they may directly affect its ability to function as a collective body as well as the ability of individual ministers to evolve and implement policies. Although these are matters for discussion in Chapter 6, it is worth noting that the one member of the Cabinet who in a sense is an exception to these considerations is the Prime Minister, who presides over ministerial reshuffles, but is not directly the subject of them. Generally speaking, the Prime Minister enjoys the longest tenure of office of all and, although some politicians survive to hold office under more than one Prime Minister – Lord Hailsham, for example, has served in four postwar Conservative Cabinets – Prime Ministers since 1945 have on average served 4.8 years in the highest office, compared with the little more than two years of most ministers in any one department. This too has important implications for the operation of the Cabinet, not least in the argument about 'Cabinet government' versus 'prime ministerial government', but it too must be left for further consideration in Chapter 6. It is important first to look at the organisation and operation of the Cabinet.

# 4 Organisation and Operation

Drawing a picture of the organisation and operation of the Cabinet is like trying to complete a jigsaw puzzle in which you do not know how many pieces there are supposed to be, except that some are missing, and in which the only guide is an earlier version of the puzzle which is itself incomplete. This is well illustrated by the efforts of MPs to secure information about Cabinet committees. Until 1979 successive Prime Ministers refused to give any information about the number and terms of reference of Cabinet committees, other than on rare occasions when, in order to demonstrate just how seriously the Government was taking a particular problem, it would announce that a special Cabinet committee had been established. In 1979, however, Margaret Thatcher was prepared to reveal that, as Prime Minister, she had

> established four standing committees of the Cabinet: a defence and overseas policy committee and an economic strategy committee, both under my chairmanship; a home and social affairs committee under the chairmanship of my rt. hon. friend the Home Secretary; and a legislative committee under the chairmanship of the Lord Chancellor. Attendance at these committees will vary according to the subject under discussion. Where appropriate sub-committees of the standing committee will be established. Members and the terms of reference of the standing committees and their sub-committees will remain confidential.[1]

In response to a similar request for information in 1970 the then Prime Minister, Edward Heath, stated:

> It has long been the practice not to disclose details of the arrangements within the government for the discussion of public business . . . not only in this Parliament but in many previous

32

Parliaments . . . I have not been able to find any occasion on which details of Cabinet committees have been publicly revealed.[2]

Unusual as Margaret Thatcher's concession was, however, it was an extremely limited one: the number of Cabinet committees is not publicly known, but it is known that it far exceeds the four mentioned in her statement. Moreover, it is not merely information about Cabinet committees that is not normally revealed, but information about the whole working of Government in general and the Cabinet in particular.

The Official Secrets Act, 1911 places severe restrictions on the disclosure of official information, whilst the law of libel ensures that the mass media are generally very careful about what information they publish. Furthermore, the operation of the lobby system by which the political or lobby correspondents of newspapers, radio and television are given privileged access to information, reinforces governmental control of information. Under the lobby system accredited journalists are given information about Government policies and about political developments, some of which may be published and its source attributed, some of which may be published but not attributed and some of which may not be published at all but is nonetheless useful for journalists to know. A serious breach of either of the latter two categories may result in the journalist concerned being denied information in the future. The lobby system has no foundation in law, but it is a powerful incentive to journalistic 'cooperation'.

Information can be a source of power and influence and it is understandable that Governments should wish to maintain a significant degree of control over the policy-making and decision-making processes, which are not necessarily always best carried on in the full glare of publicity. For example, on occasion it becomes difficult to discuss even the *possibility* of some policy proposals without arousing extremely strong feelings amongst various interests, which might inhibit a rational and sober discussion of the problem concerned. Similarly, whilst 'open agreements openly arrived at' is an admirable tenet in many respects, there are circumstances in which it is a guarantee that no agreement will be reached: however open the consequent agreement, some negotiations can only be arrived at secretly.

The leaking of confidential discussions is a well-known political tactic and the balance between secrecy and openness is not easy to strike, but it is sometimes said that British Governments are obsessed with secrecy. For instance, whether better or worse policies would emerge from Cabinet meetings whose discussions were made public is a matter of opinion, but the fact is that, under the Public Records Act, 1967, the minutes of Cabinet meetings remain unavailable for public scrutiny for a period of thirty years after the event; prior to January 1968 the period was fifty years. Apart from leaks of Cabinet discussions, ministers are therefore used to conducting Cabinet business in the knowledge that, for the most part, details of who said what, or who supported what, will remain confidential for many years, usually long after they have ceased to be ministers and possibly beyond their own lifetimes. Thus, it was perhaps not surprising that in 1975 the Government made strenuous efforts to prevent the publication of the Crossman *Diaries*, which included details of Cabinet discussions held during the Wilson administration of 1964–70. The Government sought a court injunction to prevent their publication, arguing that if it became the general practice for Cabinet discussions to be revealed ministers might feel inhibited. In giving his judgement, Lord Chief Justice Widgery said that he had not granted the injunction because sufficient time had elapsed between the time of the events described and the time of publication, but it should be borne in mind that the Government was, at this stage, seeking to prevent the publication of only the first volume of the *Diaries*, which covered the period 1964–6. Ominously, perhaps, the Lord Chief Justice said that he reserved judgement on the propriety of publishing the volumes covering later years. In the event, having lost its case, the Government did not seek to prevent the publication of the two later volumes, which, ironically, enabled a member of that very same Government, Barbara Castle, subsequently to publish her diaries for the much more recent period of 1974–6.

Whatever the pros and cons of secrecy and openness in policy-making, it is unfortunate that attempts to maintain confidentiality in the policy-making process extend in practice to information about how that process operates. The absence of information is, of course, far from total, but it is undoubtedly piecemeal and fragmented. How the Cabinet operated thirty years ago may or may not be an accurate picture of the contemporary Cabinet, whilst ministerial memoirs do not normally provide a systematic account of the operation of government. Moreover, even the Crossman and Castle diaries, which do provide a more detailed account of political events and are therefore a much richer contemporary or near-contemporary source of material on the operation of the Government in general and the Cabinet in particular, inevitably lack the systematic approach that a full understanding requires. This having been said, it is possible to draw a reasonably accurate picture of the way in which the Cabinet works, but it is important to be aware that observers are forced to rely on a variety of fragmentary sources; accounts of the organisation and operation of the cabinet are inevitably tinged with a degree of uncertainty.

It was pointed out in Chapter 3 that the Cabinet is at the top of a complex ministerial hierarchy, but it is also important to realise that the Cabinet is part of a complex administrative and decision-making machine, both in the sense that it is the political head of a bureaucratic machine – the Civil Service – and that it operates through a complex network of committees. Each departmental minister in the Cabinet is, in turn, at the head of an administrative and decision-making machine in the policy areas for which his department is responsible. The focal point of Cabinet activity, however, is No 10 Downing Street. It is here that the Cabinet normally meets; it is here that the Prime Minister normally resides and works; and it is here that the organisational centre of the Government is normally located.

As it is usually seen by the public – on television, in the newspapers or to those members of the public who congregate from time to time outside – No 10 Downing Street is deceptively small. This impression is further complicated by the fact that it is physically linked with the Cabinet Office, which is located in Whitehall. In addition No 11 Downing Street is the official residence of the Chancellor of the Exchequer and No 12 that of the Government Chief Whip; all three houses are internally linked. What then may be termed as the Downing Street complex houses the Prime

Minister's Office and the Cabinet Office, which provide administrative and organisational services to the Prime Minister and the Cabinet respectively.

The ground floor of No 10 contains the Cabinet Room and the offices of the principal members of the Prime Minister's Office. The first floor contains the Prime Minister's study, two drawing rooms, a state dining room (where official lunches and dinners are held), a reception room and the office of the No 10 Policy Unit (which is attached to the Prime Minister's Office), together with several other offices. Finally, on the second floor there is the Prime Minister's private flat. Most Prime Ministers use No 10 as their official residence in London, although during his second term of office between 1974 and 1976 Harold Wilson preferred to use his own house, then in Lord North Street near Westminster, rather than, as he put it, 'live over the shop'. In addition the Prime Minister has a country residence, Chequers, which was left to the nation after the First World War and has been used by Prime Minsters since 1921. Apart from the Prime Minister, the Chancellor of the Exchequer and the Chief Whip, two other ministers, the Lord Chancellor and the Foreign Secretary, have official residences in London and also have country residences available to them. Only in the case of the Prime Minister, however, is the official London residence 'over the shop'.

The position of No 10 Downing Street as the focal point of Cabinet activity is further complicated by the existence of the Prime Minister's Office on the one hand and the Cabinet Office on the other. Organisationally they are separate in that the former consists of the Prime Minister's immediate aides and administrative staff and the latter provides the Cabinet as a whole with various adminstrative services. As head of the Cabinet, the Prime Minister inevitably works closely with the Cabinet Office and in particular with its head, the Secretary of the Cabinet, who is a civil servant of permanent secretary rank, the highest in the Civil Service.

Both the Prime Minister's Office and the Cabinet Office are of relatively recent origin, both developing organisationally during the First World War under the premiership of David Lloyd George. Prior to Lloyd George Prime Ministers did have personal staff, the most important of whom was a private secretary, but their numbers were always limited. Furthermore, the Prime Minister's Office has always included a number of personal appointees, but in 1924 a distinction was drawn between the Prime Minister's Private and Political Office. The Private Office provides administrative services to the Prime Minister and is staffed by civil servants; the Political Office consists of personal aides and advisers.

For all Prime Ministers the role of the Political Office is to act as a liaison with the party organisation and with Government backbenchers, but some Prime Ministers also appoint one or more close political advisers. Others, however, prefer to take advice from a close friend or confidant who holds no formal post, but who can nonetheless be regarded as a member of the Prime Minister's entourage, although the tendency in recent years has been for such individuals to be given a formal post. Inevitably such individuals, whether or not they hold a formal position, become or are alleged to become extremely influential. Such influence is, of course, extremely difficult to gauge and in some cases is probably exaggerated, in others underestimated. Certainly it is often resented by other members of the Cabinet, by Government supporters in Parliament, by the party organisation – to name but a few. In practice, however, it is not always easy to distinguish between those whose advice is frequently sought and valued by the Prime Minister and those whose role is essentially that of maintaining an efficient prime ministerial organisation. More importantly, it is unrealistic not to expect most Prime Ministers to feel the need for one or more close advisers or confidants and probably unreasonable to expect that such advisers be somehow rendered publicly accountable – it is the Prime Minister who should properly be regarded as accountable, regardless of the source of any advice.

In 1964 the Prime Minister's Office had forty-five staff, but by 1975 this had risen to sixty-eight, of whom three were part-time, and in 1984 was about seventy, including a few part-time staff. The key figures in the Prime Minister's Office, however, consist of about twelve people in the Private Office and about six in the Political Office. In Margaret Thatcher's Private Office, for instance, these include the Prime Minister's Principal Private Secretary, four Private Secretaries (two of whom deal with home affairs, one with overseas affairs and one with parliamentary affairs), the Press Secretary and his/her deputy, and the Secretary for Appointments, who is concerned with seeking advice on the awarding of honours and the making of various appointments for which the Prime Minister is responsible. Margaret Thatcher's Political Office includes her Chief of Staff, who acts as a coordinator, her Political Secretary, who handles constituency and personal matters, her Personal Assistant, who is responsible for the Prime Minister's diary and daily timetable, her Parliamentary Private Secretary, who is an MP and who acts as a liaison with the party in Parliament, and two policy advisers.

The Cabinet Office is a much larger organisation and is responsible for the operation of the Cabinet as a whole, including its committees. Like the Prime Minister's Office, the Cabinet Office has grown in recent years, consisting in 1964 of 356 staff, in 1975 of 681, but falling to 547 in 1983. In the case of the Cabinet Office, however, these figures can be somewhat misleading, since the Cabinet Office includes the Central Statistical Office and a small Historical Section, which is concerned with the maintenance of Government records and, where appropriate, official histories. In addition the Cabinet Office also included the Central Policy Review Staff (CPRS), commonly known as the 'Think Tank', which was established by Edward Heath in 1970 and which, unlike the Central Statistical Office and the Historical Section, should be regarded as a potentially important part of the policy-making machinery of the Cabinet Office. As far as the Cabinet is concerned the most important part of the Cabinet Office is the secretariat, which consists of about a hundred senior civil servants. The head of the Cabinet Office is the Secretary of the Cabinet, who provides the crucial link between the Cabinet Office and the Prime Minister, who works very closely with the Prime Minister, planning and preparing the Cabinet agenda and generally overseeing the work of the Cabinet.

The Cabinet secretariat was first established by Lloyd George in 1916 and, because it originally consisted of a small staff housed in the garden of No 10 Downing Street, it became known as Lloyd George's 'garden-suburb' or 'kitchen-Cabinet'. The distinction between the secretariat and Lloyd George's personal staff was blurred, and the secretariat was therefore regarded with suspicion by Lloyd George's critics and opponents. This almost led to its destruction in 1922, when Lloyd George ceased to be Prime Minister and the size of the secretariat was reduced from 122 to 38. It survived, however, and in the early 1920s a clear distinction was drawn between the Cabinet Office and the Prime Minister's Office.

The task of the Cabinet secretariat is to prepare the agenda and circulate papers for meetings of the Cabinet and its committees, and to keep a record of the deliberation and decisions reached at such meetings. Cabinet minutes are formally known as Conclusions, which is a somewhat misleading term since they do not merely record decisions but also summarise position papers presented to the meeting and the subsequent discussion. Cabinet Conclusions are circulated to all members of the Cabinet, usually within twenty-four hours of a meeting. The minutes of Cabinet committees are also circulated, although in this case the recipients sometimes include ministers from outside the Cabinet who are members of the committee concerned. It is also the task of the Cabinet secretariat to keep track of action taken on Cabinet decisions.

It is not the task of the Cabinet secretariat to advise the Cabinet on policy matters, although there is no doubt that the Secretary of the Cabinet discusses policy with and offers advice to the Prime Minister, and in some cases the relationship between the Secretary of the Cabinet and the Prime Minister becomes particularly close. Richard Crossman suggests in his *Diaries*, for example, that such a relationship developed in the period 1964–70 between Harold Wilson and the then Secretary of the Cabinet, Sir Burke Trend (now Lord Trend).Edward Heath, however, worked particularly closely with Sir William Armstrong (later Lord Armstrong), who was Permanent Secretary of the Civil Service Department, of which, as Prime Minister, Edward Heath was formally the head.

Until the establishment of the CPRS, advice on policy matters came almost exclusively from the civil servants in ministers' departments (this still remains largely the case) but in recent years a limited number of outside advisers have been appointed. Thus, apart from one or two individuals attached to the Prime Minister's Political Office, political advisers to other ministers, or to the Cabinet as a whole, have been rare until recently. From 1964 to 1968 Nicholas Kaldor (now Lord Kaldor) was special adviser on taxation to the Chancellor of the Exchequer and from 1964 to 1967 Thomas Balogh (now Lord Balogh) was economic adviser to the Cabinet.

Between 1970 and 1974, under the Heath adminstration, six or seven ministers had political assistants paid for from party funds, whereas Kaldor and Balogh had been paid as temporary civil servants. During Heath's premiership there were also economic advisers attached to the Cabinet Office and Heath set up Cabinet Office Units to coordinate policy on particular matters. A 'Europe Unit' was established, for instance, to coordinate policy amongst the various departments during Britain's negotiations to enter the EEC, and in 1974 Harold Wilson set up a 'Devolution Unit'. The Cabinet Office Units, however, do not consist of outside advisers, but of civil servants seconded from appropriate departments. Wilson also allowed each member of the Cabinet to engage up to two political advisers and this practice was continued under his immediate successor, James Callaghan. Not all ministers chose to do so, however, and between 1974 and 1979 there were never more than forty such advisers. Margaret Thatcher also allowed the appointment of political advisers, but has limited each Cabinet minister to one adviser.

Harold Wilson was also responsible for one further innovation – the creation of a Policy Unit consisting of six or seven outside advisers attached to the Prime Minister's Office. Various observers have argued that Prime Ministers should have their own 'Prime Minister's Department' to enable their coordinating role as head of the Government to be fulfilled. It has been suggested that the Prime Minister is at a disadvantage compared with departmental ministers in the Cabinet, who have the massive resources of a Government department to brief them on departmental policies and keep them generally informed on Government policies. It is further suggested that however closely the Prime Minister works with the Secretary of the Cabinet, the Cabinet Office exists to serve the Cabinet as a whole rather than the Prime Minister in particular. Last, and by no means least, it is argued that the Prime Minister needs policy advisers from outside the Civil Service to provide not only alternative, but also 'political' advice, especially in the sense of being politically sympathetic towards the Government's policies. The No 10 Policy Unit is, at best, a small concession to this point of view; it has continued in existence on a slightly reduced scale under Margaret Thatcher.

The CPRS also had its origins in proposals for a Prime Minister's Department: in the 1960s a group of Conservatives suggested that a team of forty or fifty outside advisers, using techniques of management efficiency and cost-effectiveness, would provide the Prime Minister with continuous policy analysis and review. This team would form the kernel of a Prime Minister's Department. This and similar proposals were considered by the Fulton Committee on the Civil Service, which reported in 1968, and the possibility of establishing a policy review body was also being considered by the Labour Government before its defeat in 1970. When the CPRS was set up later that year it differed from the earlier proposals in that it was much smaller and also in being attached not to the Prime Minister's Office but to the Cabinet Office.

About half the members of the CPRS were seconded from Government departments, the other half being outsiders, mainly from universities, numbering fifteen or sixteen altogether. The first head of the 'Think Tank', Lord Rothschild, was an outsider, having been head of Shell Research prior to his appointment in 1970 and, although his successor in 1974 (Sir Kenneth Berrill) was technically a civil servant, as head of the Government Economic Service and Chief Economic Adviser to the Treasury, he had served in that post for only a short period, having previously been Chairman of the Council for Scientific Policy and of the University Grants Committee, and before that fellow of a Cambridge college.

There have been two further heads of the CPRS, both of whom were also outsiders. Sir Kenneth Berrill was succeeded in 1979 by Robin Ibbs, an industrialist from ICI, but after only two years Ibbs returned to his company and was succeeded in 1982 by John Sparrow, a merchant banker. Neither Ibbs nor Sparrow had the extensive public service experience of the first two heads of the 'Think Tank', although Sparrow had been an informal adviser to the Prime Minister and the Chancellor of the Exchequer. This lack of public experience has led to suggestions that neither was or could be effective in the complex world of Downing Street and Whitehall, but much depends upon the personality of the head. In June 1983, however, the CPRS was abolished.

The main role of the CPRS was to investigate, on its own initiative or at the request of the Cabinet or one of its committees, a lower-level departmental committee, or individual ministers, any question of policy – most usually those with medium- to long-term implications. Between 1970 and 1974 the review body also undertook six-monthly reviews of the Government's programme in relation to its 1970 election manifesto and, although such regular reviews were discontinued under later Governments, it continues to take periodic overviews of the government's strategy and priorities. Some of the reports prepared by the CPRS were subsequently published, but the majority were simply made available to the Cabinet. Apart from periodic reviews of Government policy generally, some idea of the wide range of matters with which the CPRS concerned itself can be gauged from the fact that it prepared reports on various aspects of social policy and the social services, the British car industry, energy policy, devolution, the representation of Britain abroad, race relations, regional policy, rail electrification and the control and financing of the nationalised industries.

Given the considerable secrecy which surrounds the operation of British government, it is inevitably difficult to assess the influence of bodies like the No 10 Policy Unit and the CPRS. Political advisers drawn from outside the Civil Service, whether employed individually or as part of a larger unit, have to contend with the problem of operating within the confines of a permanent bureaucratic machine – the Civil Service, which, however faithfully it may serve Governments of whatever party, is conscious that it was there before a particular Government was formed and will, short of an apocalyptic upheaval, still be there after that Government has gone. Political advisers, however, are transient members of the governmental machine and the majority are appointed as much for their political sympathies as for their expertise. They may therefore encounter resentment from civil servants, who see it as their task to advise ministers and who regard the appointment of outside advisers as a slur on their professional integrity. However, it is important to bear in mind that, apart from prime ministerial confidants, political advisers to ministers are a relatively new phenomenon in British politics and therefore not within the normal experience of senior civil servants.

In practice, much depends on the personalities involved and direct experience often quells Civil Service fears and resentment. In her *Diaries*, for example, Barbara Castle notes that the civil servants in her department were initially opposed to political advisers, but subsequently worked closely with them and welcomed them. Furthermore, some political advisers are relatively low-level appointments, acting more as personal assistants to ministers, rather than major policy advisers. For instance, Barbara Castle had three advisers, two special advisers who had specialised knowledge in the fields of health and social security and whose task was to advise her on particular policies, and one political adviser whose role was more that of a personal assistant and who briefed her on a wide range of matters, including those outside the department. Indeed, Barbara Castle found this latter role particularly valuable and used her political adviser to brief her on non-departmental matters due to be discussed in Cabinet.

There can be little doubt that particular ministers have found outside advisers useful, but there is insufficient evidence available to measure how much *influence* they have. The No 10 Policy Unit and the CPRS could similarly be described as 'useful', but again their influence is difficult to assess. In all probability they have not fulfilled the highest hopes of those who advocated their establishment and Barbara Castle records: 'I never found either the CPRS or Dr Donoughue's Unit [the No 10 Policy Unit] had any noticeable effect on the decisions we took. These depended far more on the political muscle and (expertly reinforced) political will of individual ministers.'[3] It is not possible to judge how accurate an assessment this is, although it certainly accords with the general opinion that these bodies, along with political advisers to individual ministers, have not had any dramatic influence on policy formation. The CPRS in particular has provided members of the Cabinet with a broader view of various issues than they can normally get from their departments and it may be more accurate to think of it in terms of widening horizons and *informing* rather than influencing ministers.

The No 10 Policy Unit may sometimes perform a rather different role of providing the Prime Minister with briefings on various policies in much the same way as individual advisers do for other ministers, but there is no reason to believe that it is particularly influential as such and it is important to remember that Prime Ministers need to be informed as much as, if not more than, other ministers. Above all it should be reiterated that all the political advisers, the No 10 Policy Unit and the CPRS are on a very small scale, amounting to little more than sixty individuals altogether – small beer when compared with the vastness of the Civil Service, or even senior civil servants, who number several thousands, however close they may be to the ear of the minister or even the Prime Minister. In any case, political advisers are for the most part a peripheral part of the operation of the Cabinet; far more central and vital are Cabinet committees.

Like the Prime Minister's Office and the Cabinet Office, the systematic use of Cabinet committees dates back to the First World War, and in particular to the premiership of Lloyd George, though they were not a new device then. Cabinet committees were used increasingly in the latter part of the nineteenth century to deal with particular problems or issues, the earliest examples being a committee to draft a Reform Bill in 1854 and a War Committee established during the Crimean War in 1855. After 1892 it became the regular procedure for the Cabinet to approve Bills in principle, and for the more important pieces of legislation to be referred to drafting committees drawn from the Cabinet.

In 1903 the first standing committee of the Cabinet was set up – the Committee of Imperial Defence. Unlike earlier and later committees, it included non-ministerial representatives, not only in the form of senior army and naval personnel, but also with the attendance of Arthur Balfour (Leader of the Opposition from 1906 to 1911) between 1906 and 1915, when he joined the coalition Government. The most marked expansion, however, occurred during the First World War, when the numerous committees were created to deal with matters such as shipping, control of imports, food production, military and industrial mobilisation and the development of air power. Some of these committees were inter-departmental committees of officials, others consisted exclusively of ministers. The crucial development, however, was Lloyd George's creation of a small War Cabinet of five members which necessitated the more systematic use of committees. A reduction in the number of Cabinet committees occurred after 1918, but they were now a permanent part of the organisation and operation of the Cabinet, growing in number again during the Second World War, when there was again a small War Cabinet.

The basis of the present system of Cabinet committees was established by Clement Attlee in 1945, drawing upon his experience as effective deputy Prime Minister during the war. Attlee created three types of committees: permanent or standing committees, temporary or *ad hoc* subject committees and legislative committees. Some of the committees were chaired by the Prime Minister himself, others by ministers holding sinecure posts, such as Lord President of the Council, leaving departmental ministers to speak for and concentrate on the affairs of their departments. Despite this systemisation the number of committees continued to expand and it has been estimated that by 1951, at the end of Attlee's period of office, the number of inter-departmental committees numbered at least 700, of which more than a hundred were technically Cabinet committees in that they were serviced by the Cabinet Office. In fact, in 1950 Attlee had found it necessary to establish a special section in the Cabinet secretariat to coordinate the work of committees. On his return to power in 1951, Winston Churchill's initial reaction was to avoid the extensive use of Cabinet committees, but as Cabinet business accumulated an increasing number of matters were referred to committees.

The exact number of committees in existence at any particular time is difficult to judge, since, as was noted at the beginning of this chapter, such information is not normally revealed. Nonetheless, it is possible to produce a fairly clear picture from ministerial memoirs and diaries. Richard Crossman, for example, mentions more than thirty different committees in the three volumes of his *Diaries* and Barbara Castle nearly twenty in her *Diaries*, but it is important to remember that neither sought to list all committees nor to give a systematic account of their number and operation. In his book *The Cabinet* Patrick Gordon Walker, also a former Cabinet minister, lists the number of *standing* Cabinet committees from before 1914 to 1964.[4] These range from one before 1914 to fifteen under Attlee; between seven and nine under the Conservative Governments of 1951–64 and thirteen under Wilson in 1964. However, since it is up to the Prime Minister to decide what

Cabinet committees are appropriate, the subject areas, names and number of standing committees can vary from one Government to another.

The Prime Minister may decide to reorganise Cabinet committees, as Harold Wilson did in 1967, dividing the responsibilities of the existing Economic Policy Committee amongst three new committees: one on industry, one on overseas trade and one on environmental planning, with a new Steering Committee on Economic Policy to coordinate their activities and provide strategic planning. At the same time the separate committees on defence and foreign affairs were merged to create a single Overseas Policy and Defence Committee. A number of committees are also commonly referred to by initials or acronyms. For instance, the Overseas Policy and Defence Committee is known as OPD, the committee on Rhodesia during the Wilson Government of 1964–70 was known as RX, the committee on policy towards the EEC during the Wilson Government of 1974–6 as EQ, from its title, European Questions. Where more than one committee exists in a particular area, such as economic policy, they are distinguished in a similar fashion: the Callaghan Government of 1976–9 had two economic policy committees, one known as EY – the first and last letters of the word 'economy' which dealt with overall economic policy – and the other as EY(P), which dealt with incomes policy.

Recent Cabinets have had between twenty-five and thirty committees operating at any one time, although it must be borne in mind that committees tend to proliferate during a Government's lifetime and initially every new Government tends to establish a smaller number of committees than its predecessor. Of the twenty-five to thirty, between twelve and fifteen will be standing committees, six to ten will be *ad hoc* subject committees and two or three will be dealing with specific legislative proposals. The standing committees include those on economic policy (on which more than one committee often exists) foreign affairs and defence, home affairs and social policy, and legislation. In addition, since Britain's accession to the EEC, a committee normally exists on policy towards the Common Market and, since the renewal of the 'troubles', one on Northern Ireland. Until recently there were usually two committees on legislation, one dealing with the

Government's legislative programme for the current parliamentary session and the other with planning ahead for the remaining sessions of the Parliament, but these have now been amalgamated to form a single Legislation Committee.

The various *ad hoc* committees are set up to deal with particular policies, such as those contained in the Government's election manifesto, or with problems which confront the Government during its period of office, and, once dealt with, the committee concerned is disbanded. Some such committees inevitably take on a semi-permanent nature, since the problems concerned remain unsolved or continue to need governmental attention over a prolonged period. For example, the problems of Rhodesia and devolution necessitated such committees during the Wilson and Heath Governments. Finally, all major Government policies requiring legislative action are normally referred to a Cabinet committee to examine the detailed contents of the Bill before its introduction to Parliament. Although such committees remain in existence during the Bill's passage through Parliament, they are disbanded once it has completed all its stages.

The Prime Minister chairs several of the more important Cabinet committees, leaving most others to be chaired by members of the Cabinet holding one of the various sinecure posts. Either lacking, or having minimal departmental responsibilities, such ministers are expected to take an overview of the committee's business, leaving departmental ministers to concentrate on departmental affairs. In practice, this does not prevent committee chairmen from siding with a particular department, nor does it preclude departmental ministers from taking a wider interest, but it requires an effort on their part which not all departmental ministers find it easy to make given the time consuming nature of their responsibilities.

Departmental ministers are normally members of those committees directly concerned with their responsibilities, but from time to time they may be expected to attend meetings of other committees at which matters concerning their own departments are being discussed. Some committees also include ministers from outside the Cabinet, especially where they are directly concerned with the matter under discussion; middle rank or junior ministers may also attend as substitutes for departmental heads. The

membership of committees is also subject to political considerations, particularly in terms of political balance. For example, in
1974–5, when the Labour Government was renegotiating the
terms of Britain's membership of the EEC, the European Questions Committee contained both pro- and anti-Marketeers, with
the balance slightly in favour of the former. It would, of course,
be surprising if such considerations were not taken into account,
although it remains the case that departmental representation is
the major determinant of the membership of Cabinet committees.

Cabinet committees are vital to the Cabinet: they relieve the
Cabinet of what would otherwise be an impossible burden of work
and constitute an integral part of the decision-making structure of
the Cabinet. Moreover, not only is a major part of the work on
many policies done at Cabinet committee level, but in many cases
*decisions* are made in Cabinet committees. Such decisions are
subsequently discussed in the full Cabinet only in the event of an
appeal from one or more members of the committee concerned,
or if the Prime Minister, or a sufficiently strong body of opinion in
the Cabinet favours it. Appeals from committees to the full
Cabinet were not uncommon between 1945 and 1964, but, when
he first became Prime Minister, Harold Wilson ruled that appeals
against committee decisions could be made only with the agreement of the committee's chairman. In effect this means that such
matters will receive further consideration in the full Cabinet only if
they remain substantially in dispute or are regarded as of such importance that full Cabinet endorsement is required. It is important
to remember that in many cases the question will have had a pre-
liminary discussion in Cabinet prior to being referred to a committee. Essentially the purpose of Cabinet committees is to leave the
Cabinet itself free to deal with matters that it decides are important, always bearing in mind that in this context importance is
ultimately measured in *political* rather than any other terms. Some
indication of how important Cabinet committees have become is
shown by the fact that ministers spend more time attending meetings of Cabinet committees than they do of the full Cabinet.

The Cabinet has since 1964 held a regular weekly meeting on
Thursdays, with an additional meeting being held on Tuesdays
when necessary. In the 1950s the Cabinet met twice a week, but
Harold Wilson reduced the regular meetings to once a week, and

had more work delegated to Cabinet committees, which practice has been followed by his successors. Meetings are sometimes held on other days, but usually only for special purposes, such as to discuss a major policy initiative or review progress in a particular policy area, or, of course, to deal with an emergency or crisis situation. If necessary, a small group of senior ministers, or those members of the Cabinet available, will hold an *ad hoc* Cabinet meeting to deal with any matter that requires an immediate decision. In some cases the Prime Minister, alone or in consultation with appropriate ministers, will make a decision and subsequently report the matter to the Cabinet. In addition, there is an Emergency Committee of the Cabinet to deal with day-to-day problems in the event of public service strikes, natural disasters, problems caused by severe weather conditions and so on, whilst a special committee, COBRA (its name being taken from its meeting place – the Cabinet Office Briefing Room), chaired by the Home Secretary and consisting of relevant ministers, civil servants and security advisers, deals with matters such as the Iranian Embassy siege of 1980. Meetings are generally held in the Cabinet Room at No 10 Downing Street, though they are sometimes held in the Prime Minister's room at the House of Commons – a practice not generally popular with ministers because the Prime Minister's room is not large enough to accommodate the full Cabinet in comfort. From time to time the Cabinet may also meet at Chequers (the Prime Minister's country residence) usually to review the progress of the Government's programme or to have a wide-ranging discussion on a major question of policy. Cabinet meetings are normally held in the morning, beginning at 10 or 10.30 and finishing by 1 pm.

Apart from the Secretary of the Cabinet, the Assistant and Deputy Secretaries and the Government Chief Whip, only full members of the Cabinet may attend all its meetings. The Secretary of the Cabinet and colleagues attend Cabinet in order to keep an account of its proceedings and to record any decisions made. The Chief Whip is not normally a full member of the Cabinet, but when necessary informs it about feeling amongst the Government's supporters in the House of Commons. The Chief Whip does not therefore usually play a full part in Cabinet discussions, but offers advice when consulted or, occasionally, intervenes as Robert

Mellish did in 1969 over the Government's industrial relations proposals, in order to warn the Cabinet of the strength of back-bench feeling against a particular policy. Mellish, in fact, subsequently had the unusual distinction of being made a full member of the Cabinet whilst holding the post of Chief Whip between 1974 and 1976. The Chief Whip has regularly attended Cabinet meetings since at least 1951 and previously attended only when parliamentary business was on the agenda.[5] Senior non-Cabinet ministers – especially the Government's principal legal adviser, the Attorney-General – are invited to attend those parts of a Cabinet meeting which deal with their responsibilities or where their advice is sought. In addition, middle rank and junior ministers may be invited to attend for particular items, either where the departmental head cannot attend or where they are directly concerned with the matter under discussion. In such cases, once the item concerned has been dealt with, the non-Cabinet minister leaves.

Each member of the Cabinet has a regular place at the Cabinet table: the Prime Minister sits at the centre of the long, rectangular table, with the holders of senior Cabinet posts, such as the Chancellor of the Exchequer, the Foreign Secretary, the Home Secretary, the Lord President and the Defence Secretary, sitting at the central part of the table with the more junior members of the Cabinet at its extremities. The Secretary of the Cabinet sits on the Prime Minister's right with the Secretary's two assistants at one end of the table whilst the Chief Whip sits at the other end. Richard Crossman has remarked on the advantages of a central position at the Cabinet table:

> In Cabinet the talk goes on between the Prime Minister and the Chancellor [of the Exchequer] on the one side and between the Foreign Secretary, the Home Secretary and the Defence Secretary on the other. Those in the middle talk to each other and those at the ends of the table have to shout to be heard,[6]

whilst Barbara Castle described one Cabinet meeting as

> one of those discursive chat-ins which nearly drive me mad in Cabinet. Since the main protagonists on Europe are all bunched at the other end of the table, keep turning their heads away from our end, interrupt each other and talk in low tones, it is

impossible to follow what is going on . . . In the end I gave up
. . . what they eventually decided, I haven't a clue. I just got
tired of saying, 'Please speak up'.[7]

At Cabinet meetings ministers normally address each by their
ministerial titles, although between 1974 and 1976 Harold Wilson
allowed the use of Christian names. The agenda is drawn up by
the Secretary of the Cabinet in consultation with the Prime
Minister, although there is usually a weekly review of future business at an informal meeting of senior ministers, which is also
attended by the Chief Whip and the Secretary of the Cabinet. The
Prime Minister normally chairs all full Cabinet meetings, but in
the Prime Minister's absence the chair is taken by a senior
colleague. Prior to each meeting the minutes of the previous
meeting will have been circulated by the Cabinet secretariat,
together with papers which usually form the basis of discussion at
the next meeting. Each minister is usually briefed by their own
department on each item of Cabinet business, especially where the
department's interests are affected.

The form of discussion in the Cabinet inevitably varies
according to the matters being discussed and the manner in which
the Prime Minister, as chairman, chooses to conduct Cabinet
meetings. In some cases only those ministers directly concerned
with the agenda item being discussed will contribute, in others
there is a wider discussion and on some issues the Prime Minister
may seek the views of all or most members of the Cabinet. Some
Prime Ministers, such as Clement Attlee and, it is said, Mrs
Thatcher, prefer to deal with the agenda at a brisk pace and limit
discussion to a minimum; others, such as Winston Churchill and,
at times, Harold Wilson, have allowed discussions to be discursive.
Regardless of its form, however, it is the Prime Minister who
usually sums up the discussion and who, where appropriate,
announces the Cabinet's decisions. It is rare for formal votes to
be taken in the Cabinet, other than on minor procedural matters,
although the Prime Minister may keep a note of the numbers
speaking for and against a proposal. For example, Patrick Gordon
Walker reports that 'on a number of occasions [Harold Wilson]
openly kept his own tally of the votes pro and con; and sometimes
announced the result',[8] and Crossman records three occasions

when votes were taken in the Cabinet, one of which he described as 'one of those occasions when Harold Wilson asked for individual votes'.[9]

Although the main purpose of most Cabinet meetings is to make a decision on matters on the agenda, some meetings are devoted to broader discussions of the Goverment's attitude towards a particular policy question or to a general discussion of a major issue prior to referring it to a Cabinet committee. In the latter case, for example, policy questions such as Britain's entry to and membership of the EEC, devolution and, inevitably, a variety of economic questions, have been the subject of general discussions before being passed for more detailed consideration to committees.

Economic policy generally, however, is to an important extent a special case. In particular, the annual Budget presented to the House of Commons by the Chancellor of the Exchequer is not subject to normal Cabinet discussion. The Chancellor's proposals are formulated in consultation with the Prime Minister, usually informing particular ministers about proposals which affect their departments, and then presents the whole package to the Cabinet as a *fait accompli* shortly before making the Budget speech in the House. The proposals may be briefly discussed by the Cabinet, but there is little or no time to make any substantive or significant changes and, although Barbara Castle records that in 1974 the Cabinet did persuade the Chancellor to raise the ceiling on first mortgage tax relief, it was 'the first time in my memory that Cabinet has ever influenced the Budget in any way!'[10] Moreover, it is not unusual for other decisions on economic policy to be made by the Chancellor and the Prime Minister, sometimes in consultation with one or two other senior ministers, and, even where the Cabinet is given an opportunity to discuss such proposals, more often than not it is presented with a *fait accompli*.

In 1982 a limited departure from this practice occurred. In February of that year the Cabinet was given an opportunity to discuss the Government's economic policy prior to the presentation of the Budget in March. There is no doubt that ministers were able to discuss the various possibilities open to the Chancellor of the Exchequer in forming the Budget, but there is no evidence that, as a result of this meeting, the Cabinet as a whole had any significant impact on the shaping of the Budget or on any of the Chancellor's specific proposals.

The area of economic policy in which there is rather more Cabinet influence is that of public expenditure, which is revised annually through what is known as the Public Expenditure Survey Committee or PESC, which consists of senior departmental civil servants and is chaired by a senior Treasury official. The PESC system was introduced in the early 1960s, following the presentation of the Plowden Report on public expenditure. It operates on the basis of an annual review of expenditure over a rolling three year programme. Its original purpose was to introduce more effective control over public expenditure, but in practice it has increasingly become an exercise in sharing out the 'national cake' rather than effectively reviewing the efficacy of public expenditure.

At the ministerial level, responsibility for the annual PESC exercise lies with the Chief Secretary to the Treasury, who from 1968 to 1970 and since 1977 has been a full member of the Cabinet. However, the Chief Secretary's responsibility is exercised primarily by conducting bilateral negotiations with departmental ministers once PESC has presented its package of proposals. At Cabinet level the resulting package has sometimes been dealt with by a Cabinet committee (also confusingly called PESC – in this case, Public Expenditure *Scrutiny* Committee), prior to discussion at full Cabinet. This occurred, for instance, under the Wilson Governments between 1966 and 1970 and again between 1974 and 1976. Other Governments have dispensed with the committee exercise and left the battle to be fought out in the bilateral talks between the Chief Secretary and individual ministers, and at full Cabinet.

The whole public expenditure exercise has, of course, become increasingly difficult in the face of Britain's economic performance and, although public expenditure has increased both in real terms and as a proportion of the Gross National product, ministers have more often than not been faced with making cuts in their programme rather than deciding where more money should be spent. Indeed, periodic economic crises have resulted in further cuts being made over and above those made in the annual reviews. Furthermore, from time to time Governments have been confronted with specific decisions on public expenditure, such as providing additional support to various nationalised industries and financial assistance to ailing private industries. Such questions have sometimes resulted in agonised Cabinet meetings over matters such as aid to the shipbuilding industry and meeting miners' pay claims during the Heath administration; subsidising British Steel and providing capital expenditure for British Rail under Margaret Thatcher's Government and saving British Leyland and Chrysler under both Labour and Conservative Governments. Perhaps most spectacular of all was the nationalisation of the aero-engine division of Rolls-Royce by the Conservatives in 1971. Similarly, in 1976 the Labour Cabinet had a particularly difficult meeting when it had to decide whether it was prepared to accept the conditions laid down by the International Monetary Fund in return for a massive loan.

It is also important to understand how the Cabinet deals with matters that require legislative action in the form of passing an Act of Parliament. Bills – the draft form of an act – are prepared by civil servants in the appropriate department. In the case of a measure emanating from the party's election manifesto the officials will often use the manifesto commitment and any detailed proposals produced by party policy committees as a guide or basis in drafting the Bill, and may seek fairly detailed ministerial guidance. In other cases the minister concerned may simply instruct his officials to draft a Bill designed to achieve particular objectives. Sometimes the Cabinet will have decided that legislation on the matter is necessary; sometimes the initiative is in the hands of the minister and the minister's department. In yet other cases civil servants may draw the minister's attention to the need for, or desirability of legislation, for example, the renewal of certain ministerial powers under acts such as the Prevention of Terrorism Act or the need to reorganise water authorities in the early 1970s.

All this, however, is normally preceded by a meeting before the beginning of the annual parliamentary session in October or November of the Cabinet's Legislation Committee to decide the Government's legislative priorities. Since parliamentary time is quite short, there is inevitably a limit on the number of Bills that the Government can expect to get through Parliament each session. This in turn is affected by the size, scope and complexity of each proposed Bill and the extent to which it is likely to be opposed by the opposition in Parliament. A long, complex and controversial Bill will usually take up a disproportionate amount of time and may delay or even prevent the passage of other Bills. Moreover, since parliamentary procedure does not allow a Bill that has failed to complete all its stages through both houses of Parliament through lack of time to be carried over to the next session, but stipulates that it must start afresh, the Government must plan its programme carefully and try to ensure that it does not lose control of it during the session. Whilst Governments with a secure parliamentary majority can usually get most of their legislation through Parliament, it nevertheless requires careful and skilful management.

A minority Government's legislative programme is understandably vulnerable. The minority Labour Government of 1976–9, for instance, failed to secure the passage of a motion timetabling the committee stage of its Scotland and Wales Bill in 1977 and was forced to reintroduce its proposals as separate Bills for Scotland and Wales in the following session. Even so, the minority Governments of February–October 1974 and 1976–9 managed to secure the passage of more than 80 per cent of their legislation, compared with the norm for a majority Government of well over 90 per cent. The recent experience of minority Government is not what most twentieth-century British Governments and politicians have been used to, and ministers are primarily concerned with securing the highest possible priority for their Bills rather than worrying whether they will survive their passage through Parliament. The importance of this is well illustrated by a remark reported by Richard Crossman, who quotes Herbert Bowden (now Lord Bowden) in his capacity as Lord President of the Council and chairman of the Legislation Committee, as saying: 'You needn't worry about this Bill, there won't be room for it in this session anyway!'[11]

Once the department concerned has produced draft proposals for a major Bill, it is usually referred to a Cabinet committee established for the purpose, especially if it is on a subject which affects the interests of several departments. In such cases a parallel committee of officials from the department concerned is established to discuss detailed proposals and present these to the Cabinet committee. Major legislative proposals may also be preceded by the publication of a White Paper outlining the proposals, which will necessitate a line-by-line approval of the White Paper at a full Cabinet. Before embarking on its passage through Parliament, a Bill is checked for drafting errors by the Cabinet's Legislation Committee and a date is set for its first reading – the first of its parliamentary stages.

Most Government legislation is introduced in the Commons first rather than the Lords, although the latter house is used first for dealing with some non-controversial Bills and for what are known as consolidation Bills, which bring together under a single statute legislation in a particular field. The first reading is a formality which marks the publication of the Bill, so that its first substantive stage in Parliament is its second reading – the purpose of which is to discuss the principles or broad proposals of the Bill. This is followed by the committee stage, at which the Bill is discussed clause by clause, usually in a standing committee of some fifteen to twenty MPs, but occasionally on the floor of the House, in which case any MP may participate. There then follows the report stage at which any amendments made in committee are reported to the House and finally the Bill receives a third reading, at which a final look is taken at the whole Bill before it proceeds to a similar process in the other house.

Generally speaking, the Cabinet has little to do with a Bill once it has embarked on its passage through Parliament, although it, or one of its committees, may consider the Government's attitude towards amendments proposed at the committee stage and, occasionally, may have to decide whether an amendment made in committee should be reversed on report, at the third reading, or in the Lords. Apart from this the minister whose department is promoting the Bill normally makes the major speech on the Bill at second reading. Responsibility for the Bill during its committee and later stages is normally taken by the minister or one of the minister's junior ministers.

The operation of the Cabinet is determined not only by its organisation and the matters with which it has to deal, but also by its composition. It was noted earlier that the position of ministers at the Cabinet table can affect their participation in Cabinet meetings. Similarly, their role in the work of the Cabinet is affected by their membership of Cabinet committees. Another factor of considerable importance is the distinction between departmental and non-departmental ministers. Most departmental ministers are

kept extremely busy by their departmental responsibilities. Both
Richard Crossman and Barbara Castle have commented on this.
Crossman remarked that being a departmental minister makes it

> very much easier to remain the kind of minister who doesn't
> play much of a role in Cabinet. It keeps my reading of Cabinet
> papers down . . . I don't often look at Foreign Office telegrams
> . . . [12]

and Barbara Castle comments on one occasion,

> As for myself, I was barely listening. Iceland is peripheral to my
> own concerns. Nor had I really time to master the Chrysler crisis
> . . . [13]

Conversely, Crossman points out that in 1970 Peter Shore, in his
capacity as 'Minister-without-Portfolio', demonstrated the advantage of non-departmental ministers with time to read Cabinet
papers by being able to bring about the withdrawal of the Chancellor of the Exchequer's economic assessment paper for 1970–2,
which had been presented to the Cabinet's Steering Committee on
Economic Policy.[14]

More importantly, departmental ministers are not only kept
busy by their departments but tend to concentrate mainly on
departmental business in Cabinet, as Barbara Castle illustrates:

> We . . . all fought passionately for our own [legislative] bids
> again. It was a fight with no quarter given by anyone;[15]

and

> Another of those wretched PESC Cabinets . . . Everyone
> fought his corner.[16]

The fact that the Cabinet consists of individuals should never be
forgotten. Much that occurs in Cabinet depends on the personalities of those individuals, the offices they hold and also their
tactical skill in getting Cabinet approval for their department's
proposals and in negotiating support for them amongst Cabinet
colleagues. Again, as Crossman remarks,

> one should always be looking for friends and allies, not making
> enemies. That's why a Cabinet minister is reluctant to weigh in
> on too many things,[17]

and failure to do so may have unfortunate consequences:

> [Anthony Greenwood, Minister of Housing and Local Government] got massacred in the last PESC cuts by having no friends.[18]

Above all, these individuals are politicians and, whilst most of them have administrative duties, as members of the Cabinet they constitute not so much part of an *administrative* machine but part of a *political* machine: in short, the Cabinet is a focal point of political activity in British politics.

# 5 The Cabinet at Work: Case Studies

To describe the life of a Cabinet minister as 'busy' is an understatement. Furthermore, it is not merely that ministers invariably work long hours and, especially in the case of departmental ministers, have a considerable burden of paperwork, but that they are expected to deal with an enormous variety of matters. The overwhelming impression from ministerial memoirs in general and from the Crossman and Castle *Diaries* in particular, is that ministers, both individually and collectively, are expected to slip from one subject to another with bewildering rapidity.

Barbara Castle, then Secretary of State for Health and Social Services, described Wednesday, 2 July 1975, as 'one of the busiest days of my ministerial life'. It began with a meeting of the Cabinet committee on devolution. This was followed by a meeting at Barbara Castle's department with representatives of the British Medical Association. A quick sandwich lunch was preceded by a brief visit to the hairdresser, prior to opening a new day hospital for the mentally ill. Later in the afternoon Barbara Castle appeared before the Select Committee on Violence in Marriage at the House of Commons. This left her half-an-hour to change for dinner, during which time some of her officials and one of her outside advisers arrived with the latest draft of a document on the social wage. The dinner (which was to celebrate the Queen's birthday) was held at Hampton Court and on the way Barbara Castle began to go through the boxes of official papers which ministers receive every day. After the dinner she returned to her London flat to find one of her political advisers waiting with another urgent document. In anticipation of yet another busy day she set her alarm for 6.30 am.[1]

Lest it be thought that Barbara Castle's day was totally exceptional, it is instructive to look at a week in the life of a Cabinet minister. In this case the minister concerned is Richard Crossman and, in order to broaden the picture, three separate weeks have been chosen, one from each of the periods he served in different ministerial offices, first as Minister of Housing and Local Government, then as Lord President of the Council and Leader of the House of Commons, and finally as Secretary of State for Health and Social Security.

## Minister of Housing and Local Government, 5–11 December 1965

*Sunday, 5 December*: Crossman spent the day at Prestcote, his farm in Oxfordshire, mainly going through his 'red' (official) boxes and discussing the organisation of his department with a senior civil servant.

*Monday, 6 December*: Crossman travelled from Prestcote to London and spent the morning discussing the Rent Act with civil servants. In the afternoon he prepared a speech on the Rating Bill, of which he moved the second reading in the House of Commons that evening.

*Tuesday, 7 December*: He attended a Cabinet meeting in the morning at which Rhodesia, wage-related and unemployment sickness benefits, the future of the Fairfield (Glasgow) shipyard and housing subsidies were discussed. The last item was Crossman's responsibility. In the afternoon Crossman held a press conference at his department on industrialised building, followed by a second conference at the House of Commons on coastal preservation. In the evening Crossman was guest speaker at the annual dinner of the Farmers' Club.

*Wednesday, 8 December*:  In the morning Crossmen met with Fred Willey, Minister of Land and Natural Resources, and some of his officials, to discuss a proposal to use Ullswater in the Lake District as a source of water for Manchester. This was followed by lunch with a number of friends and journalists. He spent the afternoon with George Brown, Secretary of State for Economic Affairs, discussing the need for housing subsidies with a deputation of Labour MPs and councillors from Liverpool. In the evening Crossman and his wife invited friends to dinner.

*Thursday, 9 December*: Crossman received a message from Dame Evelyn Sharp, his permanent secretary, asking him to discuss an urgent matter with James Callaghan, Chancellor of the Exchequer. He saw Callaghan as they arrived for a Cabinet meeting. The Cabinet discussed the Fairfield shipyard question again and ex-officio JPs. Crossman does not record what he did in the afternoon. In the evening he held what was to become a regular weekly meeting with James Callaghan, at which they discussed informally various matters, including Rhodesia, building societies and the economy. Crossman also attended another regular weekly meeting – a dinner with Marcia Williams (now Lady Falkender), Harold Wilson's Political Secretary, Tommy Balogh (economic adviser to the Cabinet) and others, held at the house of Tony Benn, the Postmaster-General. On this occasion they discussed strategy for the General Election that they anticipated would be called by Harold Wilson before too long.

*Friday, 10 December*: Crossman went by train to Swansea, where he addressed students at the University College and then held a public meeting. After a buffet supper and discussion with Swansea city councillors, Crossman returned to London by the night train.

*Saturday, 11 December*: Crossman returned to Prestcote and spent the day preparing for a farm supper to be held in the evening. At the supper he was lobbied by some of his guests about the local village school.

*Lord President of the Council and Leader of the House of Commons 2–8 April 1967*

*Sunday, 2 April*: This was the last day of the Easter parliamentary recess and Crossman spent it on holiday at Prestcote.

*Monday, 3 April*: Crossman travelled to London and had an informal discussion with Harold Wilson and John Silkin (the Government Chief Whip) on the *Torrey Canyon* – the oil tanker which had gone aground off the Scilly Isles – the Bristol–Siddeley affair in which the aero-engine firm had been criticised by the Public Accounts Committee of the House of Commons for making excessive profits on engine overhauls, and on reform of the Lords and the Commons. In the afternoon he attended a meeting of the

Cabinet's Home Affairs Committee to discuss a Private Member's Bill on hearing aids and in the evening went to a dinner at No 10 for Hubert Humphrey, then Vice-President of the United States. After the dinner Crossman had an informal and unplanned meeting with Tony Benn (now Minister of Technology), Peter Shore (Parliamentary Secretary at the Ministry of Technology), and Tommy Balogh.

*Tuesday, 4 April*: The morning began with a meeting of the Cabinet's Legislation Committee, of which Crossman was chairman. This was followed by a Cabinet meeting devoted to a discussion of prices and incomes policy. Crossman had lunch with his family in the revolving restaurant in the Post Office Tower and then went to the House of Commons to hear Wilson speak in the *Torrey Canyon* debate. Crossman did not record what he did in the evening.

*Wednesday, 5 April*: Crossman spent part of the morning with his children and this was followed by an informal meeting of ministers on the Bristol–Siddeley affair, prices and incomes and the *Torrey Canyon*. He spent most of the afternoon listening to a debate in the Commons; had a short meeting with Wilson about the Private Member's Bill on hearing aids and then attended a meeting of the Labour Party's Liaison Committee, which acted as a link between the Parliamentary Labour Party and the Government. In the evening Crossman felt unwell and went home to his London flat.

*Thursday, 6 April*: Crossman attended the regular weekly Cabinet meeting which was devoted to a major discussion of Britain's proposed entry to the Common Market. In the afternoon Crossman made his weekly statement to the House of Commons on parliamentary business for the following week and then had a discussion with Wilson on the future of Tommy Balogh, who was seconded from his post at Oxford University. Crossman spent the evening preparing a ministerial broadcast on the Parliamentary Commissioner for Administration (the Ombudsman), whose office came into operation in April 1967.

*Friday, 7 April*: The morning was first taken up with a meeting with the Lord Chancellor on the reform of the House of Lords, followed by a meeting of the Home Affairs Committee to discuss sonic booms and, finally, a meeting with Yigal Allon (a member of the Israeli Cabinet) and the Israeli Ambassador on arrangements for the celebration of fiftieth anniversary of the Balfour Declaration of 1917. Crossman does not record what he did in the afternoon, but in the evening he had a discusssion with Tommy Balogh and his wife about Balogh's future.

*Saturday, 8 April*: This was spent electioneering for Greater London Council elections in North London suburbs.

### Secretary of State for Health and Social Services, 12–18 October 1969

*Sunday, 12 October*: Crossman spent the day at Prestcote, having invited Sir Jock Campbell – a businessman and chairman of the *New Statesman and Nation* publishing company and a long-standing Labour supporter – and Tommy Balogh, to lunch. They discussed the latest Cabinet reshuffle and other Government changes and Campbell asked Crossman if he was interested in becoming editor of the *New Statesman*.

*Monday, 13 October*: In the morning Crossman had a meeting with representatives of the TUC on some details of the proposed new National Pension Scheme. This was followed by a meeting with one of his senior civil servants and then Crossman had a working lunch with Brian O'Malley and John Dunwoody, two of his recently-appointed junior ministers. After lunch Crossman attended part of a debate on Northern Ireland, but left to address a Labour Party meeting in Battersea on his superannuation proposals.

*Tuesday, 14 October*: The morning was devoted mainly to a Cabinet meeting at which Northern Ireland and the current dustmen's strike were discussed; but the major business was discussing what should be included in the Queen's Speech – the outline of the Government's programme for the new parliamentary session due to begin shortly. Immediately after the Cabinet meeting Crossman had a short meeting with Wilson about a number of public lectures he had been asked to give. Crossman then had lunch with Peregrine Worsthorne, a leading journalist on the *Sunday Telegraph*. In the afternoon he chaired a departmental meeting with representatives of the Pharmaceutical Society on the price of drugs. That evening Crossman and his wife gave a dinner for John Dunwoody and his wife, Gwyneth, who was also an MP.

*Wednesday, 15 October*: Crossman spent the morning preparing for a press conference on the establishment of the National Health Service Hospital Advisory Service and the appointment of its first director. The press conference was held at lunch-time and was followed by a meeting of the Overseas Policy and Defence Committee of the Cabinet to discuss the export of the Chieftain tank to Israel. Crossman does not record what he did in the evening.

*Thursday, 16 October*: The early part of the morning was devoted to a continuation of the Overseas Policy and Defence Committee meeting of the previous day, which was followed by a full Cabinet meeting dealing mainly with the Chancellor's PESC proposals for 1971–2. Crossman's superannuation proposals were briefly discussed before the meeting finished. In the afternoon Crossman travelled to Canterbury to give a talk to the University of Kent Labour Club and in the evening he addressed a public meeting in Dover – the constituency of David Ennals, Crossman's Minister of State at the Department of Health and Social Security.

*Friday, 17 October*: Early in the morning Crossman rang David Ennals to discuss Ennals' appearance on the BBC's 'Panorama' Programme the following Monday. Later in the morning he visited a hospital and then had lunch with Julian Snow, MP, one of his junior ministers. In the afternoon Crossman went to Coventry, where he was one of the local MPs, to talk about the social services to students at the University of Warwick. He then spent the weekend at Prescote.

In his *Diaries* Crossman does not, in fact, record every happening of every day and sometimes does not relate what he did for, say, a whole afternoon or evening, occasionally omitting a whole day. Indeed, there is one occasion when Crossman reports,

> I can't say anything about this because I was sound asleep. I do sometimes sleep in Cabinet but I've never failed to wake up before we reach my item on the agenda.[2]

Nonetheless, a sufficiently clear picture emerges and two important impressions are gained from looking at the *Diaries* over a
period of time. First, regardless of whether a minister is a departmental or non-departmental minister, he is expected to deal with
a great variety of matters. Thus, in the week relating to his period
as Minister of Housing, Crossman mentions no less than thirteen
different subjects which were the subject of discussion within his
department, or with other ministers, or in the Cabinet. Similarly, twelve matters were covered during the week taken from his
period as Lord President and nine as Health and Social Services
Secretary. Within the Cabinet itself discussions also varied widely,
with four subjects in the first week, two in the second and four
again in the third. Second, if a distinction is drawn between
Crossman's role as an individual minister and as a member of the
Cabinet, a clear difference emerges between the departmental and
non-departmental roles. As an individual departmental minister
Crossman dealt almost exclusively with matters for which his
department was responsible, even in his discussions with ministerial colleagues, whereas as Lord President he ranged much more
widely. Of course, as Lord President Crossman was a member
of a wide range of Cabinet committees, some of which he
chaired.

It is not merely that departmental ministers tend to be busier
– this too is clear from the three weeks reviewed above, but it is
part of the role of non-departmental ministers to range more
widely as members of the Cabinet. At the same time, departmental ministers are not necessarily precluded from dealing with
matters outside their departmental remits, but their departmental
duties do not leave them much time for dealing with wider matters
– even as members of the Cabinet. Crossman's excursions outside
his departmental responsibilities tended, in fact, to be informal in
nature, reflecting Crossman's own inclinations and wider interests
rather than that which was expected of him. In some cases,
however, a departmental minister may be deeply involved in a
policy area outside his department because he has been deliber-
ately involved by the Prime Minister or because he formerly dealt
with the matter. When he was Secretary of State for Health and
Social Services, for example, Crossman continued to be deeply
involved in the attempt in 1968–9 to reform the House of Lords,

since it was he who, as Lord President, had been responsible for the original proposals.

A clearer picture of the policy-forming process itself can be gained from examining several policies through their various stages, again using the Crossman *Diaries* as a source. What follows does not purport to be a complete picture of the policy-making process (a task which is beyond the scope of this book) so much as a sketch of how Crossman dealt with two particular matters in his department and presented them to the Cabinet. This is followed by two other examples, one where Crossman was chairman of the Cabinet committee concerned with the problem and the other where he had no direct responsibility for the matter under investigation. First, the two issues for which Crossman had responsibility as a departmental minister.

## The Rent Act, 1965

In 1957 the Conservative Government passed a Rent Act, the purpose of which was to allow the rents for private, unfurnished accommodation to rise nearer to their market level. Prior to the act they had been subject to Government control. The 1957 Act was bitterly opposed by the Labour Opposition, but, as Crossman pointed out, when he took office as Minister of Housing,

> although the Labour Party has been committed for five years to the repeal of the [1957] Rent Act, there is only one slim series of notes by Michael Stewart [Shadow Minister of Housing before the 1964 Election] on the kind of way to do it in the files of Transport House. Everything else has to be thought up on the spot.[3]

As soon as he took office in October 1964, Crossman discussed the question of legislating on rents with his Permanent Secretary, Dame Evelyn Sharp (now Lady Sharp), who had prepared some notes on the subject prior to the election.

The preparation by senior civil servants of proposals designed to implement the policy commitments of the main Opposition party *before* it has actually won office at an election is common practice and is not regarded as a sign that the Civil Service necessarily expects the governing party to lose the election; nor is it frowned upon by the Government, but it was something which took a number of the incoming Labour ministers by surprise in 1964.

It was clear that the 1957 Act could not simply be repealed, since it *decontrolled* rents and, therefore, some new method of determining the level of rents had to be devised. It was also the purpose of Labour's policy to give tenants substantially greater security of tenure, especially after what became known as the Rachman scandal had focused attention upon the problem of the exploitation and eviction of tenants in the Notting Hill area of London. Furthermore, one of the later criticisms of the 1957 legislation was the lack of consultation of various outside interests that had preceded its enactment,[4] and Crossman was determined that adequate outside consultations would take place, especially to achieve a workable solution to the problem of assessing rents.

Crossman's civil servants in the Ministry of Housing and Local Government pointed out that such consultations, the devising of suitable machinery and the passage of a relatively long Bill through Parliament, would be a fairly lengthy process and therefore advised him to separate the question of immediate security of tenure from the questions of longer-term security and the regulation of rents. They proposed a short, one-clause Bill giving tenants security of tenure pending the passage of the main Rent Bill, a proposal which Crossman accepted and presented to the the Legislation Committee of the Cabinet at the end of October 1964, which was approved by the Committee early in November. The resulting Protection from Eviction Bill was not discussed in full Cabinet and proceeded to a fairly swift passage through Parliament, receiving the royal assent on 17 December 1964.

In the meantime, the Legislation Committee considered Crossman's proposal for a more detailed Rent Bill in the context of the Government's whole legislative programme and gave it first priority in that session's major pieces of legislation. Crossman then set about evolving the detailed proposals necessary to implement his policy by establishing two discussion groups in his department. One group was headed by himself and Arnold Goodman (now Lord Goodman), who had acted as a legal adviser to a number of Labour MPs (including Harold Wilson),and the other jointly by James MacColl, Parliamentary Secretary at the Ministry of Housing, and David Donnison, Professor of Social Administration at the London School of Economics. At the beginning of December Crossman held a departmental policy session on ways of defining a fair rent and subsequently sought the views of members of the Milner Holland Committee, which had been set up by Crossman's Conservative predecessor to investigate problems associated with the Rachman scandal. Although the committee was unable to complete its report before the passage of Crossman's legislation through Parliament, they were able to give the minister useful advice, notably that his Bill should include furnished accommodation. However, Crossman's officials persuaded him to reject this advice because they would not be able to complete the drafting of the Bill to facilitate its early passage through Parliament.

The two discussion groups established by Crossman produced a number of proposals, but these were omitted from a paper prepared by the department's civil servants for presentation to the Cabinet. However, on Crossman's insistence the Cabinet paper was redrafted and the discussion groups' proposals were incorporated. These proposals were then discussed in a meeting between Crossman and the National Association of Property Owners. The paper was presented to and received the approval of the Cabinet after a brief point-by-point discussion on 18 November 1964.

Although the Cabinet had approved Crossman's proposals, consultations on various details continued with outside interests. For example, one issue that had to be resolved was that of tied cottages, which is the provision of unfurnished accommodation as part of a job – especially important in farming. Negotiations to solve this problem were conducted with the National Farmers' Union and the National Union of Agricultural Workers.

In March 1965 a White Paper outlining the proposals and the resultant Bill were published. Crossman held a special meeting with journalists to explain the policy and a further meeting to explain the Bill to Labour MPs. The Rent Bill had its formal first reading in the House of Commons on 23 March 1965. Its first substantive parliamentary hurdle – the second reading – took place on 5 April 1965, with Crossman leading the debate for the Government. The committee stage of the Bill, in which it was examined clause by clause, took place between 13 April and 30

June. Although the Conservative Opposition opposed the Bill, Crossman negotiated a timetable for its committee stage with the leading Opposition spokesman on the standing committee dealing with the Bill. During the committee stage Crossman met with Labour members of the standing committee to discuss its progress and to listen to their misgivings about some of its provisions. Initially Crossman himself led for the Government on the standing committee, but for most of the committee stage James MacColl was the Government spokesman. Following various representations made during the committee stage, eight new clauses and fifty amendments were tabled by the Government. The Bill's report stage (at which an amended Bill is again presented to the full House of Commons) took place on 30 June and the final Commons stage, the third reading (giving the House a final opportunity to consider a Bill) took place on 6 July. In both cases the Opposition had agreed a timetable for the Bill's passage. The Bill now proceeded to the House of Lords where it received its second reading on 8 July. The committee stage in the Lords, however, was not finally completed until October because of the summer recess. Some changes were made in the House of Lords, but none that caused any clash between the two Houses and the Rent Bill received the royal assent on 8 November and came into operation one month later.

Meanwhile, Crossman had used the recess to plan the administrative machinery necessary to implement the Bill's proposals, notably the appointment of rent assessment committees and rent officers, and the preparation of advertising to make the public aware of the new provisions for determining security of tenure and rents in unfurnished accommodation.

### The National Superannuation and Social Insurance Bill
The second case is that of reforming the national pension or state superannuation scheme. The Labour Party had been discussing the whole question of pensions since the 1950s, and in 1957 Crossman, as the member of the Labour Party's National Executive Committee responsible, had announced plans for a new national pension scheme at the party's annual conference. In essence, the proposals sought to replace the existing flat-rate pension scheme with an earnings-related scheme. However, not

only was the whole question of pensions extremely complex and therefore required an extensive period of consultation and preparation, but the Labour Government elected in 1964 had other, more urgent, legislative priorities. Thus, although a number of discussions on pensions were held at Cabinet committee level in the first two and a half years of the Wilson administration, it was not until March 1967 that a Cabinet Pensions Committee was established.

At this time Crossman was Lord President of the Council and, partly because it was one of the Lord President's functions to chair a number of Cabinet committees – but more particularly because of his long involvement with and knowledge of pensions – Crossman became chairman of the committee. A parallel committee of civil servants had already been established and Crossman secured the Prime Minister's permission to have some officials attending the Cabinet committee, since pensions was such a complicated subject. Crossman wanted to have a new pension scheme in operation before the next election, due in the Spring of 1971 at the latest, but officials at the Ministry of Pensions and the Treasury counselled delay given the complexities of the subject. They favoured a Bill passed through Parliament in 1969 or 1970, with the first contributions paid into the scheme in 1972 or 1973 and the first benefits paid out in 1974, but Crossman made every effort to secure earlier implementation. A short delay occurred early in the policy-making process because the then Minister of Social Security, Margaret Herbison, resigned from her post in protest over increases in the prices of school meals and milk, and her replacement, Judith Hart, needed time to familiarise herself with the subject of pensions.

Nonetheless, discussions amongst officials continued and Crossman was informed by civil servants that the change to earnings-related contributions would require extensive new computer facilities which would not be available for three years. As before, Crossman pressed on, but by December 1967 he felt that the officials' discussions were delaying progress and, with Wilson's approval, decided that the whole question would be taken over by the Cabinet Pensions Committee, which officials would no longer attend. Crossman himself embarked on a series of discussions with representatives of outside bodies, particularly the CBI and the

TUC, and, as he had done with the Rent Bill, established a discussion group involving outside advisers – in this case Brian Abel-Smith and Richard Titmuss, both Professors of Social Administration at the London School of Economics; Tommy Balogh, economic adviser to the Cabinet; and, from time to time, Nicholas Kaldor, economic adviser to the Chancellor of the Exchequer. This group, which Crossman dubbed 'the circus', met with the other ministers and civil servants involved and 'a real policy began to emerge'.[5]

In April 1968 Crossman ceased to be Leader of the House of Commons and, though retaining for the time being the post of Lord President, became coordinating minister for the Ministries of Health and Social Security, pending their merger into a single department later that year. Crossman therefore assumed departmental responsibility for the superannuation proposals and in October 1968 became Secretary of State for Health and Social Security.

Inevitably a major concern on the superannuation policy was the cost of the scheme which involved complex negotiations with the Treasury at both official and ministerial levels, but by the end of July 1968 the Social Services Committee of the Cabinet (which, unlike the Pensions Committee, was concerned with the wider implications of the scheme) had approved the basic scheme. Further consultations occurred during August and September, the agreement of the Chancellor of the Exchequer was secured, the Prime Minister being kept informed of progress. Early in October the Social Services Committee gave its approval to the detailed scheme that had been worked out and on 17 October Crossman presented his scheme to the Cabinet. His presentation and the subsequent discussion – mainly between Crossman and Roy Jenkins, the Chancellor – lasted forty-five minutes. The proposals were discussed at two further Cabinet meetings, but in both cases the item was low on the agenda and not much time was devoted to it. At the third meeting, on 31 October, the Cabinet approved the scheme, but Crossman was forced to concede biennial rather than annual reviews of contributions and benefits.

By mid-November a draft of the White Paper, *National Superannuation and Social Insurance: Proposals for Earnings-Related Social Security* (Cmnd 3883, January 1969), was being circulated in Government departments prior to presentation to the Cabinet's Social Services Committee and to the Cabinet itself. As with all White Papers, it was subsequently examined by the Cabinet line-by-line. Meanwhile, Crossman made various provisions for publicising the proposals, including seeking the advice of Hugh Cudlipp (now Lord Cudlipp), then Chairman of the International Publishing Corporation (owners of the *Daily Mirror*), and briefing a number of Labour MPs interested in pensions. On the day of publication Crossman held a press conference and appeared on television, whilst simultaneous press conferences were held in Edinburgh and Cardiff. On 30 January Crossman explained his proposals to the Parliamentary Labour Party's backbench committee on social security. Although reactions were favourable, only eight people attended the meeting. The proposals were debated by the Parliamentary Labour Party on 20 February and, although strongly opposed by the Conservatives, the Government had no difficulty in securing their approval by the House of Commons on 6 March.

Meanwhile, consultations on the details of the scheme were continuing, particularly over the question of individuals already covered by private pension schemes partially contracting out of the state scheme. These consultations continued during the summer and were not completed until the autumn of 1969. Among those consulted were the CBI, the TUC, representatives of occupational pensions funds, ICI and NALGO.

The drafting of the Superannuation Bill continued throughout this period and the Cabinet's Social Services Committee held its first meeting on part of the Bill in May 1969. In July a further White Paper was published – this time on short-term benefits under the scheme. Extensive negotiations with the Treasury were also necessary to work out the details of contracting-out proposals and the funding of the scheme, especially the level of employers' contributions. Cabinet approval of the contracting-out arrangements was given in September, but the negotiations with outside interests ran into difficulties and the question came before the Cabinet again early in October. A White Paper on the contracting-out arrangements was eventually published at the beginning of November.

At the end of October a further problem arose when, at a

routine meeting of the Cabinet's Home Publicity Committee, it emerged that the Treasury, the Inland Revenue and the newly-created Civil Service Department had all failed to consider the question of 'over-pensioning', ie, the level at which tax concessions on pensions were withdrawn. Moreover, the Treasury now regarded the proposed level of employers' contributions as insufficient and wished to increase it from $6\frac{3}{4}$ per cent to 7 per cent. Eventually a compromise was reached on both matters; that on employers' contributions necessitated the introduction of further legislation to increase National Health Service contributions.

Crossman was now busy planning publicity for the National Superannuation Bill and began by holding a large public meeting with 2000 delegates from NALGO, whose members had a major interest in the proposals. There was some delay in the Bill being dealt with by the Cabinet's Legislation Committee because Crossman was ill with 'flu, but plans were eventually made for the Bill's second reading to take place early in the New Year. The Bill had its first reading on 16 December 1969 and the second reading was moved by Crossman on 19 January 1970. Privately Crossman had been assured by the Conservative spokesman on pensions that his party did not oppose the Bill in principle, but wished to amend some of its detailed provisions. The Commons standing committee appointed to take the committee stage of the Bill had its first meeting at the end of January and, despite good progress and Conservative assurances, Crossman expressed the view that a guillotine or timetable motion would probably be necessary to enable the Bill to complete its committee stage on schedule. Although Crossman occasionally attended the committee, the task of piloting the Bill through the committee stage was left to his ministerial colleagues at the Department of Health and Social Security. The committee stage of the Bill was still in progress, however, when the Prime Minister advised a dissolution of Parliament, so that not only was the National Superannuation Bill unable to complete its passage, but it became one of the casualties of the General Election of 1970.

The other two cases are the question of the devolution of governmental powers to Scotland and Wales, following the growth of electoral support for the nationalist parties in those parts of the

United Kingdom, and the introduction of British Standard Time in 1968. Crossman was closely involved in the first, since he was chairman of the Cabinet committee on devolution, but involved in the second merely as a member of the Cabinet.

*Devolution*

In July 1966 Gwynfor Evans, President of Plaid Cymru (the Welsh National Party) won the Carmarthen by-election and focused attention on the question of nationalist feeling in Wales and, later, in Scotland. Reinforced by the fact that the Labour Party had a substantial lead in the opinion polls, there was a tendency by some members of the Government to attribute the Carmarthen result to special factors, such as the popularity of the former Labour MP, Lady Megan Lloyd-George, the effectiveness of Gwynfor Evans as a candidate, the relative strength of support for the nationalist cause in rural Wales and the general weakness of the Conservatives in Wales. In March 1967, however, in two further by-elections, the Plaid Cymru came second in the poll at Rhondda West and the Scottish National Party (SNP) won sufficient votes in Glasgow (Pollok) to enable the Conservatives to win the seat from Labour. Then, in November 1967, Labour lost the normally safe seat of Hamilton to the SNP. The nationalist threat now began to be taken seriously.

Richard Crossman was interested in the growth of nationalist support for several reasons: first, as Minister of Housing and Local Government until August 1966, he was responsible for plans for local government reform; second, as one of the Labour Party's electoral strategists and tacticians, he was concerned with the threat the nationalist parties presented to Labour's electoral strength in Scotland and Wales; and, third, as Lord President of the Council, he subsequently became chairman of a Cabinet committee seeking ways of dealing with the nationalist threat. Indeed, Crossman mentions in his *Diaries* that, late in 1966, he raised the question with the Prime Minister. It was not until May 1967, however, that serious consideration was given to the matter, when the Home Affairs Committee of the Cabinet discussed proposals for the reform of local government in Wales. Crossman favoured a more ambitious proposal for the establishment of an elected Welsh Council or Parliament, but found little support.

In November 1967, in his capacity as Lord President, Crossman discussed the whole question with John Mackintosh, Labour MP for Berwick and East Lothian and former Professor of Politics at the University of Edinburgh; David Marquand, Labour MP for Ashfield and a former Lecturer in Politics at the University of Sussex; and David Owen, Labour MP for Plymouth (Devonport). Mackintosh, in particular, favoured the devolution of legislative and executive powers to Scotland and Wales, and Crossman took the view that devolution would undermine support for the nationalists, who wanted independence for Scotland and Wales, and help Labour electorally. In addition, Crossman saw devolution as part of a wider package of local government and regional reform. He therefore established a Scottish working party, chaired by Mackintosh, to produce a policy on devolution.

It was not until March 1968, however, that a Cabinet committee on devolution, with Crossman as chairman, was set up. Initially, the committee concentrated on Wales, in spite of the fact that the SNP presented a much more serious electoral threat to Labour than did the Plaid Cymru. This appears to have been done for two reasons: first, because proposals for changes in Wales had already been formulated and presented to another committee and, second and more importantly, because William Ross (the Secretary of State for Scotland) and the Scottish Labour Party were strongly opposed to any form of devolution. This was partly reflected in the composition of the Devolution Committee which included Cledwyn Hughes, the Secretary of State for Wales, whereas Scotland was represented by Dickson Mabon, MP, a Minister of State at the Scottish Office, rather than by Ross himself. This in turn led to only limited proposals to meet the nationalist challenge in Scotland, involving procedural changes in the House of Commons rather than conceding any form of devolution. These proposals included making greater use of the Scottish Grand Committee (which could deal with various items of exclusively Scottish parliamentary business), creating an additional Scottish standing committee to take the committee stage of Scottish legislation and setting up a Select Committee on Scottish Affairs. These proposals were discussed by the Devolution Committee in April 1968.

The local government elections in May 1968 showed further gains by the SNP, but not by the Plaid Cymru, and Crossman

became increasingly concerned about the nationalist impact in
Scotland. The Government then found itself upstaged by the
Conservatives when Edward Heath proposed an elected Scottish
Assembly and a constitutional committee on the reorganisation of
government in Scotland. Crossman, however, continued to face
strong opposition in the Cabinet to any proposals for devolution
and there was only a lukewarm reaction to the procedural
proposals presented by the Devolution Committee in June 1968.
Crossman favoured the appointment of a royal commission on
self-government in Scotland as a reply to Heath's proposals, but
the Prime Minister suggested that Crossman discuss the whole
question further with the Secretaries of State for Scotland and
Wales.

The Devolution Committee had also been considering more
administrative devolution to Scotland and Wales, and this was
received more favourably by the two Secretaries of State. Since
there were already royal commissions at work on local government
reform in England and Scotland and the Government had already
published proposals for Wales in 1967, it was agreed that any
devolution proposals should be linked with local government
reform in time for proposals to be included in the Labour Party's
manifesto for the next election, due in early 1971 at the latest.

In July 1968, however, the nationalist threat in Wales was
re-emphasised by the Caerphilly by-election, in which a Labour
majority of more than 21,000 was reduced by the Plaid Cymru to
less than 2,000. The pressure for a royal commission built up and,
after two Cabinet discussions in October 1968, it was agreed that
a commission should be established. The intention to set up the
Commission on the Constitution was announced in the Queen's
Speech at the end of October, but its terms of reference were not
announced until February 1969; its membership until April 1969;
and its report was not presented until 1973, by which time Labour
was no longer in office. Subsequently, of course, devolution was
to become a major issue, following a further increase in support
for the nationalist parties in the two elections of 1974, and was
ultimately to be the issue which brought about the defeat in the
House of Commons of the Labour Government of James
Callaghan in 1979.

*British Standard Time*

In June 1967, following a proposal from the Home Office, the Cabinet's Home Affairs Committee agreed to the introduction of British Standard Time, which, by adopting time one hour ahead of Greenwich Mean Time, would bring Britain into line with her Western European neighbours. Only those members of the committee representing Scotland opposed the proposal since it meant that in the middle of winter it would not get light until 10 am in the north of Scotland, compared with 8 am in southern England. A week later the Cabinet gave its approval, again opposed by William Ross, Secretary of State for Scotland. However, it was also agreed that the position should be reviewed after three years; British Standard Time was therefore introduced on 18 February 1968.

Initially the impact was limited, since the change was made only some weeks earlier than the usual change from GMT to British Summer Time (also one hour ahead of GMT), but by November 1968, when the clocks had *not* been put back an hour as usual, the change began to make its full impact. Naturally, the impact increased the further north one went and was especially unpopular in Scotland, as Ross had predicted. It was in these circumstances that, without consulting the Cabinet, the Home Secretary, James Callaghan, announced in a speech in Scotland in December 1968, that the position was to be reviewed at the end of that winter. His announcement was not repudiated by the Cabinet or by the Prime Minister and in April 1969 the experiment was reviewed, but the Cabinet decided that the original three-year period should be completed. British Standard Time continued to be unpopular and was abandoned in October 1971, following a free vote in the House of Commons.

What sort of picture of the Cabinet emerges from the brief outlines of ministerial life and the four case studies? The short answer is that it is a complex rather than a simple picture. In particular, it is clear that the Cabinet is only a part of the governmental system, not merely in the sense described earlier as part of a governmental hierarchy, but also in terms of *policy-formation*. Indeed, there are times when the role of the Cabinet in the formation of policy could only be described accurately as minimal. This clearly calls for elaboration and comment, and on more detailed examination a number of features are revealed which place the position of the Cabinet more clearly in the policy forming process.

First, as has already been noted, ministers are expected to deal with a great variety of matters, even within the confines of a particular department and even more so as a member of the Cabinet. It is therefore clear that they cannot normally settle one problem at a time both as departmental and Cabinet ministers. Of course, they can concentrate more on one issue at the expense of others, but their working days and work patterns are inevitably fragmented. This has the obvious advantage that in dealing with one issue, sight is not lost of other – perhaps more important – issues, and it is important that the impact of a policy on other issues is taken into account. Thus, one of the major functions of the Cabinet is to act as a coordinating body in relation to the whole range of Government policies. On the other hand, dealing with a number of issues at once can be a distraction, and departmental ministers may be tempted to concentrate on their departmental affairs. In any case, it is not difficult for them to become largely immersed in the affairs of their own departments. As a result they may not only find it difficult to pay adequate attention to those issues which fall outside their departmental responsibilities, but also see such issues from a basically departmental view rather than a broader, governmental point of view.

Second, and closely connected with the first, there is the question of *priorities*. All Governments have their priorities, some of which stem from their ideological and partisan commitments, others which are thrust upon them. A newly-elected Government will, of course, be committed to a number of policies listed in its election manifesto and, in all probability, will claim it has an electoral mandate to implement them. These policies will normally be given the greatest priority, but for a variety of reasons they cannot necessarily all be implemented at once or even quickly. Some policies require a simple, straightforward action on the part of the Government, others require detailed planning and discussion; some require no legislative action, others require the passage of possibly long and complex legislation through Parliament. For example, following the General Election of February 1974 the incoming Labour Government did not require legislative action to settle the miners' strike, which had been largely responsible for precipitating the election, the settlement of which the new Government made its first and most urgent priority. On the other hand, the commitments to change trade union law and to nation-alise the aircraft and shipbuilding industries required legislative action which had to be preceded by detailed discussions with those interests involved. Similarly, the commitment to renegotiate Britain's terms of entry to the EEC required extensive discussion within the Government and with other members of the Commu-nity. Moreover, as already pointed out in Chapter 4, the Govern-ment must decide its legislative priorities, given the practical limits on the number of Bills that Parliament can cope with in each parliamentary session or year. In 1964, for instance, the Labour Government's legislative priorities were Crossman's Rent Bill, leasehold reform and the establishment of a Land Commission to control the profits from land development. In the event, both leasehold reform and the Land Commission were delayed, mainly because of the complexities of the subject, and legislation was not introduced until after the General Election of 1966.

There are other matters with which the Government must deal that they either cannot or do not anticipate. The sudden and drastic rise in oil prices following the Arab–Israeli war of 1973 was not anticipated and presented the Conservative Government of Edward Heath with a problem which inevitably affected a wide range of Government policies. One of the Government's responses was to create a separate Department of Energy, headed by a senior minister with a seat in the Cabinet. Similarly, Harold Wilson's Labour Government had to decide what, if any, response it should make to the growth of support for nationalist parties in Scotland and Wales between 1966 and 1970. In this case, a Cabinet committee was set up, but it is clear from the brief discussion earlier that the matter was not given a very high priority and was eventually passed to a royal commission for investigation. It was a different matter in 1974, however, when the increased electoral support and, more particularly, parliamentary representation won by the SNP and the Plaid Cymru, forced the minority Labour Government to consider devolution as a major priority.

A third feature that emerges from examining the work of the Cabinet is the role of the Civil Service. It would indeed be surprising if the Civil Service did not play a major role in policy formation, but some politicians and other observers have gone so far as to argue that it is the civil servants rather than the ministers who dominate the policy-making process. This is often put into a simplistic form, as if the choice is either bureaucratic or ministerial domination, when in reality it is more complex. Certainly, the opportunities exist for civil servants to frustrate a Government's proposals, but it can be argued that this is a legitimate role to the extent that it is the task of the Civil Service to ensure the practicability of the Government's policies. On superannuation, for instance, Crossman reported that his officials wished to proceed more slowly because pensions were such a complex matter and later raised the problem of adequate computer facilities. It is also the case that civil servants in particular departments come to favour some proposals and not others; a 'departmental policy' on certain issues may therefore exist, but this is hardly surprising, since civil servants inevitably acquire a considerable degree of specialised knowledge which may well lead them to favour particular courses of action. On the 1965 Rent Bill, for example, officials preferred their own proposals to those made by the discussion groups established by Crossman, but changed the draft proposals when instructed to do so by the minister.

The evidence to support the view that the Civil Service engages in the wholesale obstruction of Government policies is difficult to assess. A number of former Cabinet ministers, including Richard Crossman and Barbara Castle, but perhaps most forcefully, Tony Benn, have claimed experience of varying degrees and forms of Civil Service obstruction, whilst, on the contrary some Conservatives have claimed to detect a pro-Labour bias amongst civil servants. However, the evidence is piecemeal and fragmented, tending to demonstrate that on particular issues departments can and do resist ministerial views, on the one hand, and seek to impose departmental views, on the other; but such evidence falls short of the view that ministers are the prisoners of their civil servants. Of more importance are several other factors, for example, the extent to which the minister's life is organised by officials can create a situation in which he can be cut off from the real world, or at least important parts of the real world. As Crossman put it:

It's the black cars, the Departments, the standing in Parliament, buoying us up and insulating Ministers against shocks to an extraordinary degree. Every now and again the real world impinges on us but only when Whitehall and Westminster politics require it to do so.[6]

Furthermore, the constant pressure under which ministers work, the need to deal with immediate and pressing problems and a continuing flow of decisions, inevitably strengthens the position of the civil servant vis-à-vis the minister. As long ago as 1924, following the formation of the first Labour Government, the Prime Minister, James Ramsay Macdonald, recorded in his diary that he was able to understand

> how officials dominate Ministers. Details are overwhelming and Ministers have no time to work out policy with officials as servants; they are immersed in pursuing business with officials as masters.[7]

There is also the question of how long a minister holds a particular office. It was noted in Chapter 3 that, on average, ministers hold a particular office for just over two years and some observers, including Crossman, have argued that too short a tenure of office weakens the ability of the minister to control policy within his department:

> Too many job changes . . . means a tremendous decline in the power of the politician over the Civil Service machine and a tremendous growth in the power of the Whitehall Departments, both to thwart central Cabinet control and to thwart departmental Ministers' individual control . . . a Minister needs eighteen months to get real control of his department. I had just about got it when I was moved from Housing and therefore I was deprived of the third and fourth year when I could really have achieved something. Harold [Wilson] has appointed Denis Healey for a five-year period and he probably has done a great deal to change the detailed running of Defence.[8]

Others, such as Enoch Powell, have argued that ministers should be concerned not so much with acquiring an intimate knowledge of departmental policies and responsibilities, as with providing political impetus and direction, and that a competent minister will have done all he can usefully do in that respect within eighteen months. Finally, it is all too easy (and the temptation may be especially strong once a former minister is back in Opposition) to blame civil servants for what may have been a failure of the minister or of the policy. Nor should it be forgotten that Governments and ministers have to make decisions within the constraints of the real world, whereas Oppositions may happily dwell in a hypothetical world. It remains a matter of opinion whether civil servants have 'undue' influence over policy, but in the complex modern world it is unrealistic to expect ministers who, in most cases, have no particular expertise in matters for which they are constitutionally and politically responsible, either as departmental ministers or members of the Cabinet, to evolve policies without the specialised advice of civil servants. It therefore follows that those civil servants will have a significant influence over policy formation.

The argument about the overall role of the Civil Service tends to obscure its more mundane role in the detailed formation of policy. It was pointed out earlier in this chapter, for example, that it was Crossman's officials in the Ministry of Housing who persuaded him to introduce a separate Protection From Eviction Bill in order to provide protection for tenants pending the passage of the main Rent Bill, and to omit furnished accommodation from the latter's provisions. In the case of the National Superannuation Bill Crossman goes so far as to describe a senior civil servant variously as 'the brains behind the whole pension plan', 'the foster-parent of the scheme' and 'really the brains and foster-nurse of the whole pensions scheme'.[9]

It is also important to bear in mind, as was pointed out in the case of the Rent Bill, that the governing party may know what it wants to achieve but may not have evolved any particular means of achieving it. Another excellent example of this is the Labour Party's desire to implement its 1964 election pledge to help mortgage holders, as Crossman relates: 'Once it was clear that I was determined to put our pledge into practice, the Department was extremely resourceful and Brain [a senior civil servant] and the Dame [Evelyn Sharp, Permanent Secretary at the Ministry of Housing] thought up the ingenious idea of the option mortgage',[10] which provided for fixed interest payments for borrowers with limited income tax liabilities. These are, of course, particular examples, but it should be stressed that within each Government department detailed policy formation is largely in the hands of civil servants and, that where a Cabinet committee is responsible for a particular policy a parallel committee of officials exists to work out the details of the policy at inter-departmental level. The significance of inter-departmental committees of civil servants is aptly summarised by Crossman:

> I have yet to see a Minister prevail against an inter-departmental official paper without the backing of the Prime Minister, the First Secretary [head of the former Department of Economic Affairs] or the Chancellor [of the Exchequer].[11]

A fourth feature of the working of the policy-making process lies outside Government departments – the importance of outside interests, usually in the form of pressure or interest groups. Consultation over Government policies is widespread but haphazard. Glimpses of it are seen in the accounts of the Rent Bill and the National Superannuation Bill. In a limited number of cases particular groups or interests may have a statutory or legal right to be consulted, whilst in other cases there is a strong tradition of consultation, but neither amounts to a guarantee that such consultations will be adequate. Circumstances vary, but factors such as the extent to which the Government needs the expertise that outside interests can provide to formulate a workable policy, or the extent to which the subsequent operation of the policy depends on the cooperation of outside interests, may lead to extensive consultation. On the other hand, the Government may be aware that the outside interests oppose its proposals and see little point in consulting them, or offers of consultation may be spurned. In practice, there is no set pattern, no systematic machinery for consultation in general, and the influence of such interests may be considerable or minimal.

The last and perhaps most striking feature of the way in which the Cabinet works is that there are occasions when it appears to deal cursorily with particular matters. Crossman provides several examples of this. On the decision to adopt British Standard Time, for instance, Crossman commented:

> It is one of those reforms we gaily accepted in Cabinet in half-

an-hour, against the mutterings of Willie Ross who said it would be deeply unpopular in Scotland . . .[12]

and on reform of the House of Lords:

> We got Lords' reform through in eight minutes, the tactics and the whole White Paper. It was curious, a whole elaborate piece of reform agreed when they have never really read it. It is something that happens in our Labour Cabinet.[13]

It sometimes depends where a matter happens to be placed on the Cabinet agenda, as Crossman points out several times in respect of his complicated pensions proposals, noting on one occasion:

> Then we came to my pension scheme, late on the agenda for the third week running. It was now 12.00 and I won because it was so late.[14]

And on another occasion:

> We had gone on a good long time so no proper time was left to consider my abatement White Paper. I have great luck, because National Superannuation always comes at the end of Cabinet, they don't understand it and they never have time to discuss it.[15]

Nor should it be thought that Cabinet committees are immune:

> This afternoon the Social Services Committee met under my Chairmanship and my complete pension plan went through without any serious questioning except from James Callaghan, who after being Chancellor [of the Exchequer] knows a great deal about it . . . No one looked at the main economic impact of the scheme, its social impact or its effect on women or its effect on trade unions. All that was left to the Ministry in charge.[16]

> My only big committee was Tony Crosland's [Secretary of State for Local Government and Regional Planning] Local Government, to deal with the Maud [Committee] recommendations [on local government], the biggest administration-shattering proposals put forward in the last five years . . . The Committee has clearly been briefed by the civil servants to deal with depart-

mental interests . . . It's staggering how little serious discussion there has been of the basic principles.[17]

Ministers are under considerable pressure, of course, and departmental ministers come under particular pressure to concentrate on matters that affect the interests of their departments, but there is a more fundamental reason: the Cabinet is not part of a clear-cut process which is easily translated into a flow chart and its role varies from one matter to another. To say, for example, that all important matters are discussed by the Cabinet, let alone decided by it, begs the question, for it is a matter of judgement as to what is important. The Cabinet may spend a great deal of time discussing a matter because the Prime Minister and colleagues consider it important, not because it will necessarily affect millions of people or cost millions of pounds. Conversely, a matter which does affect millions of people and costs millions of pounds may be dealt with briefly simply because the Cabinet is content with what has been reported to it and is prepared to leave the matter primarily in the hands of the minister responsible. This should not be regarded as an abdication of its duty, but an indication of its varying role.

John Mackintosh has accurately described the Cabinet as a 'coordinating body and Court of Appeal',[18] by which he meant that it coordinates the work of departments by determining the Government's priorities and acts as a final arbiter in the event of inter-departmental disputes over policy. By so doing it seeks to give the Government's policies a significant degree of coherence. In performing this task, however, it may be more accurate to talk of the Cabinet *system* rather than of the Cabinet as a body, since it is difficult to consider the working of the Cabinet without considering the work of its individual members and their subordinates – both ministerial and official – and the network of Cabinet and inter-departmental committees which are an essential part of that system.

Nevertheless, a vital gap in the picture remains – the role of the Prime Minister. Apart from attendance at Cabinet meetings and those Cabinet committees which are chaired by the Prime Minister, in the brief accounts of Crossman's ministerial life the Prime Minister is mentioned a number of times, but does not figure as prominently as might be expected. This is not merely because the accounts of prime ministerial life or of particular issues are seen through Crossman's eyes, but because it is an accurate reflection of much that occurs in the formation of public policy in Britain: where, then, does the Prime Minister fit into the picture? What is the relationship between the Cabinet and the Prime Minister? Does Britain have Cabinet government or prime ministerial government? It is to these questions that the final chapter is addressed.

# 6 Cabinet or Prime Ministerial Government?

> The post-war epoch has seen the final transformation of Cabinet government into prime ministerial government.[1]

Thus wrote Richard Crossman in his Introduction to a new edition of Walter Bagehot's *The English Constitution* in 1963. It is important to realise that Crossman wished to emulate Bagehot, as he makes clear in the introduction to the first volume of his *Diaries*:

> my ambition was to write a book which fulfilled for our generation the function of Bagehot's *English Constitution* a hundred years ago . . . It could only be done by someone who knew party politics from the inside, and that must include council politics, parliamentary politics and if possible the politics of Whitehall and No 10.[2]

Crossman was, in many respects, well-suited to his self-appointed role: he had been a university teacher and served as a local councillor before the Second World War, he had spent the war years in Whitehall and had been a backbench MP much involved in Labour Party politics from 1945 to 1963 when he became Labour's frontbench spokesman on education, and then, in 1964, became a member of the Cabinet. He had kept, more or less regularly, a detailed diary between October 1951 and the end of 1963[3] and, on assuming ministerial office in October 1964, he resumed keeping his diary. His diaries, particularly those covering his time as a minister, were the raw material with which he intended to fulfil his ambition, but it was not to be, for, sadly, Crossman died before he could complete the editing and publication of his diaries. The diaries were published posthumously and constitute a major source of our knowledge of the workings of British government in general, and the Cabinet in particular. The diaries are also a contemporaneous account of the life of the 1964–70 Labour administration seen through Crossman's eyes, punctuated with periodic but not systematic comments by Crossman. Moreover, although Crossman did give his views on the question of prime ministerial government in a more systematic form in the Godkin Lectures he gave at Harvard University in 1970,[4] these views were fairly hastily assembled whilst Crossman was still a busy member of the Cabinet and could not really be described as his considered views on the subject. Exactly what Crossman would have said about prime ministerial government had he been able to produce a reflective, considered modern equivalent of Bagehot is a matter for speculation, but there is no reason to believe that he would have departed from his basic thesis that Britain now had prime ministerial rather than Cabinet government. In his Introduction to Bagehot Crossman actually went further:

> With the coming of prime ministerial government, the Cabinet, in obedience to the law that Bagehot discovered, joins the other dignified elements in the Constitution.[5]

It could, of course, be pointed out that Crossman wrote this *before* he had had any experience as a member of the Cabinet, but after six months' experience he wrote in his *Diaries*:

> the analysis I made in the Introduction to Bagehot is being confirmed. Certainly it is true that the Cabinet is now part of the 'dignified' elements in the constitution, in the sense that the real decisions are rarely taken there, unless the Prime Minister deliberately chooses to give the appearance of letting the Cabinet decide a matter.[6]

John Mackintosh, author of the major contemporary work on the Cabinet, was certainly prepared to go some way down the same road as Crossman, agreeing that '. . . the politics of the 1960s have strengthened rather than weakened or altered the lines of development which have led contemporary British Government to be described as prime ministerial rather than Cabinet government',[7] but adding that 'Crossman goes too far'[8] in assigning the Cabinet to a 'dignified' role in the British system of government. Leaving aside the position of the Cabinet for the moment, how can the position of the Prime Minister best be described?

A description commonly used is that of *primus inter pares* – first among equals – often in order to assert that though this may once have been the case, it no longer is. The phrase appears to have been taken out of context, however. It was used by Lord Morley, a member of all Liberal Cabinets between 1886 and 1914 and biographer of Gladstone, in his biography of Sir Robert Walpole, although it should be noted that he was discussing the position of the Prime Minister as he saw it towards the end of the last century:

the Prime Minister is the keystone of the Cabinet arch. Although in Cabinet all its members stand on an equal footing, speak with an equal voice, and, on the rare occasions when a division is taken, are counted on the fraternal principle of one man, one vote, yet the head of the Cabinet is primus inter pares, and occupies a position which, so long as it lasts, is one of exceptional and peculiar authority.[9]

Morley was stressing the equality of membership of the Cabinet in terms of *discussion* rather than ultimate power, and arguing that the Prime Minister is in fact a very powerful figure. It is likely that members of Cabinets in Morley's day would have disputed his assertion of the equality of all members of the Cabinet, other than the Prime Minister, even in discussion, and members of more recent Cabinets most certainly would. There is little doubt that both in terms of offices held and individual personalities, some members of the Cabinet are considerably more powerful and influential than others. Moreover, it is clear from the comments of three recent holders of the office of Prime Minister that members of the Cabinet in general are clearly subordinate to, and less powerful than, the Prime Minister:

*Sir Anthony Eden* (*later Lord Avon*) (*Prime Minister 1955–7*)

A Prime Minister is still nominally *primus inter pares*, but in fact his authority is stronger than that. The right to choose his colleagues, to ask for a dissolution of Parliament and, if he is a Conservative to appoint the chairman of the party organisation, add up to a formidable total of power.[10]

*Sir Alec Douglas-Home* (*now Lord Home*) (*Prime Minister 1963–4*)

Every Cabinet Minister is in a sense the Prime Minister's agent – his assistant. There's no question about that. It is the Prime Minister's Cabinet, and he is the one person who is directly responsible to the Queen for what the Cabinet does.

If the Cabinet discusses anything it is the Prime Minister who decides what the collective view of the Cabinet is. A Minister's job is to save the Prime Minister all the work he can. But no Minister could make a really important move without consulting the Prime Minister, and if the Prime Minister wanted to take a certain step the Cabinet Minister concerned would either have to agree, argue it out in Cabinet, or resign.[11]

*Sir Harold Wilson* (*Prime Minister 1964–70 and 1974–6*)

Every Prime Minister's style must be different, but I find it hard to resist the view that a modern head of government must be the managing director as well as the chairman of his team, and this means he must be completely *au fait* not only with developments in the work of all main departments, including the particular responsibility of No 10, but also with every short-run occurrence of political importance.[12]

That the Prime Minister is a powerful figure, indeed the most powerful figure in the British system of government, no one would deny. Furthermore, there can be little doubt that the power of the Prime Minister has increased considerably since the office of Prime Minister became an established part of that system. However, some care should be taken to distinguish between the extension of governmental activity, which, by increasing the power of the Government, has also increased the power of the Prime Minister, and the extent to which the Prime Minister's power has increased within the context of the governmental system, particularly vis-à-vis the Cabinet. This can be done by considering the advantages enjoyed by a modern Prime Minister.

The Prime Minister is normally the acknowledged leader of a major political party that has an absolute majority of seats in the House of Commons. The Prime Minister effectively appoints all other members of the Government and has considerable additional powers of patronage in the form of peerages, honours and various paid and unpaid appointments with which supporters may be rewarded both inside and outside the Government. The Government of which the Prime Minister is head is sustained by strong party cohesion or discipline in the House of Commons and, although the position of leader is open to challenge, any opponents within the party could expect to replace their leader only in circumstances of exceptional dissatisfaction with the leadership, unless the Prime Minister chooses to retire or is forced to resign through ill-health. Not only does the Prime Minister appoint ministers, but he or she may dismiss them, either singly or as part of a wider Government reshuffle. The Prime Minister is chairman of the Cabinet, has considerable control over its agenda and determines what Cabinet committees shall exist and who their members shall be. Lacking departmental responsibilities, the Prime Minister can concentrate on the general supervision of government policies or intervene in the affairs of any department, using personal staff and those of the Cabinet Office. The media – press, radio and television – pay far more attention to the activities and pronouncements of the Prime Minister than to those of any other politician in the country, with even more such attention being focused on the Prime Minister during a General Election. Moreover, the Prime Minister has the right to recommend a dissolution of Parliament and therefore also the power to decide when an election will be held, whilst the advent of opinion polls provide the Prime Minister with the means of deciding the most propitious moment to call an election. It has also been argued that, by the manipulation of policy in general and of economic policy in particular, the Prime Minister can create a favourable atmosphere for an election.

To point out that these advantages have not always existed merely reinforces the view that the position of the Prime Minister has become more powerful. Nonetheless, it should not be forgotten how heavily the power of the Government in general, and of the Prime Minister in particular, rests on the two-party system, which has been the norm for more than a hundred years. Of course, during that hundred years there have been periods when the dominance of the two-party system has been interrupted or modified by party splits or the increased electoral support and parliamentary representation for third parties. In some instances this has resulted in periods of minority Government, in which a single party has formed an administration but has been dependent upon other parties in the House of Commons for its survival. This occurred following the two elections of 1910, for example, when Asquith's Liberal Government was sustained by the support of the Irish Nationalists and the Labour Party, in 1923–4 and 1929–31, when minority Labour Governments were sustained by Liberal votes, and, most recently, from February to October 1974 and 1976–9, when first Harold Wilson's and then James Callaghan's minority Labour Governments lived a hand-to-mouth existence until a parliamentary agreement was concluded with the Liberals in March 1977. Minority Government inevitably limits the power of the Government and therefore of the Prime Minister, since there is usually a price to pay for the support of other parties and, not only may the Government be forced to make concessions to those who sustain it in power, but it can no longer be certain that most of its legislative programme will be enacted. At the same time, a minority Government retains the executive power and the very considerable powers of initiative in Parliament that belong to any Government.

Much therefore depends upon the party system. Indeed, were the party system to undergo a dramatic change through increased support for a new party, such as the Social Democratic Party, or for the Liberal – Social Democratic Alliance, with or without the assistance of a change in the electoral system, the operation of the British system of government could be considerably altered. In particular, if a change in the party system were to result in coalition Government becoming the norm, then significant changes in the position of the Government and the Prime Minister could result. A coalition would involve bargaining *within* the Government, both on its formation and during its life, rather than *between* the Government and other parties which support it in Parliament, as is the case with minority Government. A Prime Minister would have to form a Government from members of not only his or her own party, but from the party (or parties) of his or her coalition partners – a considerable limitation of choice. The Prime Minister could not necessarily be certain that favoured policies could be carried through the Cabinet and the House of Commons. The power of dismissal and the power of dissolution would be similarly circumscribed.

In practice, much would depend on what sort of changes occurred in the party system and what sort of Governments resulted from those changes. Nonetheless, the position of Prime Minister would remain extremely powerful, but is this position as powerful as it is sometimes suggested? Are there limits on the power of the Prime Minister beyond those that apply to the Government as a whole?

The constraints under which a Prime Minister operates in choosing the members of the Cabinet were extensively discussed in Chapter 3 and it is clear from that discussion that the Prime Minister is far from having total freedom of choice. Ministers must normally be MPs or, in a limited number of cases, peers. As leading figures in the Prime Minister's party most are already experienced career politicians. Consideration must be given to party representation and to the political and administrative skills required to form an effective Cabinet. Much the same may be said of power of dismissal: used skilfully it can strengthen the Cabinet by removing deadwood, bringing in new ministerial talent and giving new impetus to the Government's activities, but it can also be damaging to the reputation of the Prime Minister, as it almost certainly was to that of Harold Macmillan in 1962, when, in what became known as the 'July massacre', he sacked a third of his Cabinet and made twenty-four governmental changes altogether. In such circumstances it was inevitable that it should have been asked whether it might not have been more appropriate for the Prime Minister himself to go.

The power of appointment and dismissal however, can be, and is, used by the Prime Minister to shape the general and specific direction of policy, as Mrs Thatcher demonstrated in September 1981 when she reinforced her Government's commitment to its economic policy by dismissing several so-called 'wets' and transferring James Prior from the Department of Employment to the Northern Ireland Office. On the other hand, as it has already been suggested, too frequent Cabinet reshuffles may weaken ministers' control over their departments and this may in turn weaken rather than strengthen the position of the Prime Minister.

The Prime Minister's party is also a source of prime ministerial strength, sustaining, as it does, the Prime Minister in office, but it too can be a constraint on prime ministerial power. The party is the principal channel of political advancement and outside lies the political wilderness. Indeed, that wilderness can extend into the ranks of the party, for failure to win the favour of the party leader, or the loss of that favour once won, may all too easily frustrate the ambitions of the would-be minister, the minister hopeful of promotion, or the former minister, just as easily as self-exile. As Richard Crossman cynically remarked in his *Diaries*, as long as Hugh Gaitskell was leader of the Labour Party he did not expect to achieve ministerial office should Labour win power, but, 'as Harold Laski used to remind us, in British politics while there is death there is hope. Gaitskell died and Harold Wilson succeeded him. My prospects were transformed.'[13] The ambitious politician must work through the party, but the Prime Minister must be able to retain the support of the party. The idea that British political parties will follow the party leader in any direction for no other reason than that he or she is leader of the party, does not bear close examination: the party leader who loses touch with the feelings of the party imperils his or her own position.

It is, of course, notoriously difficult to overthrow a party leader, all the more so if he or she holds the office of Prime Minister. The rumblings of discontent and revolt are by no means uncommon, but the successful overthrow of a leader by his or her party is rare. Only four party leaders this century – Arthur Balfour in 1911, Austen Chamberlain in 1922, Sir Alec Douglas-Home in 1965 and Edward Heath in 1975 – have been rejected by their parties in Opposition. Similarly, only three Prime Ministers – H. H. Asquith in 1916, David Lloyd George in 1922 and Neville Chamberlain in 1940 – have lost office as a result of a failure to retain the confidence of their supporters. It could also be argued that both Sir Anthony Eden and Harold Macmillan (who resigned as Prime Minister in 1957 and 1963 respectively) would have been forced to resign in any case, had not ill-health intervened. In Eden's case the evidence is inconclusive though strong, but in Macmillan's all the evidence suggests that he would have remained in office had his health permitted. There is also the unusual case of Ramsay Macdonald who, in 1931, remained Prime Minister with Conservative and Liberal support when he was unable to persuade the bulk of his own Labour Party to support him.

It should never be far from the observer's mind that, for the most part, the major political parties in Britain exist to win political power in order to implement their policies and they therefore choose leaders who they judge are most likely to fulfil that aim. Once having chosen a leader and won power, they do not lightly overthrow that leader and risk the loss of power; nor is the prospect of winning power often put at risk by discarding a leader during a period of Opposition. This inevitably enhances the power of the leader in general, and of the Prime Minister in particular, but it does not amount to prime ministerial government. The rarity with which party leaders are overthrown lends facile support to the view that continuance in office is a sign of the total subordination of the party to the leader. However, such a view ignores the strenuous efforts that party leaders have to make to maintain party unity and offer a credible alternative to their opponents, in and out of office.

The major parties in Britain are frequently described as 'broad coalitions', a description which they often apply to themselves, and the range of views contained within their respective ranks do not permit total domination by the leader's views. In Government the pressure upon the Prime Minister to pursue policies which will ensure the party success at the next election increases inexorably as that election looms closer, whilst in Opposition the leader is under similar pressure to accept policies which will lead to the winning of power. They are not, of course, the only pressures or even, necessarily, the most important ones, but they exist and are taken into account. The leader of a party which has lost an election comes under particular pressure to adopt policies different from those previously pursued by the party, as Edward Heath found after electoral defeats in 1966 and 1974, and Hugh Gaitskell and Harold Wilson found after defeats in 1959 and 1970 respectively. The relationship between Prime Minister and party is not a simple one of leader and led, but an infinitely subtle one in which, on occasion, the leader may find it necessary to follow rather than lead, in which leadership means persuasion rather than direction, and in which clear limits exist on the policies which may be adopted or pursued.

Of course, the Prime Minister can use the extensive powers of patronage to sustain his or her position, both within the party and the Government: loyal supporters can be rewarded with peerages and other honours, with appointments to various boards and commissions and, for those with legal qualifications (common amongst MPs), with various judicial appointments. That abuse of the powers of patronage has occurred from time to time, especially in the past as a means of securing contributions to party funds, cannot be denied. It is equally true that loyal supporters of the Prime Minister are rewarded through the powers of patronage, but as a means of sustaining the position of the Prime Minister patronage in terms of honours and appointments is of limited use. Ironically, the growing volatility of electoral feeling in the 1960s and 1970s has made Prime Ministers particularly wary of rewarding members of the House of Commons in a way that creates by-elections, since all too frequently for comfort the subsequent by-elections have been lost. In practice, patronage is one of a number of factors which contribute to the party cohesion or discipline which ultimately sustains the Prime Minister in power. Much the strongest basis for that cohesion is the desire to see the party's policies implemented, a desire normally shared by the Prime Minister and his or her supporters in Parliament and in the country, for most of whom a poor Government formed by their party is infinitely better than a good Government formed by their opponents.

It is sometimes said, however, that persistent rebels amongst MPs run the risk of having their political careers destroyed by the withdrawal of party support at an election. Certainly the loss of the party label is likely to be a fatal handicap: all the available research evidence suggests that most of the electorate votes for parties rather than individuals and the fate of those MPs who have sought re-election without the backing of one of one of the major parties reinforces this view. That the withdrawal of party support is a weapon available to the Prime Minister gained credibility, even notoriety, when Harold Wilson, as Prime Minister and party leader, warned members of the Parliamentary Labour Party in March 1967 in the following terms, after more than sixty Labour MPs had abstained in a Commons vote:

All I can say is 'watch it'. Every dog is allowed one bite, but a different view is taken of a dog that goes on biting all the time. If there are doubts that the dog is biting not because of the dictates of conscience but because he is considered vicious, then things happen to that dog. He may not get his licence renewed when it falls due.[14]

The fact that Wilson subsequently described this as 'a throw-away reference' which elicited 'literally no reaction in the meeting . . . apart from some mild amusement',[15] is hardly relevant, given the interpretation placed upon it then and since. Yet there is no doubt that the power of the national party organisation or of the Prime Minister to secure the withdrawal of the party label from a sitting MP is extremely limited. The selection of parliamentary candidates, and therefore the re-adoption of sitting MPs, is largely a matter of local party autonomy. It is true that from time to time particular MPs have had official party backing withdrawn, but it has seldom been at the instigation of the national party organisation or the party leader. MPs are, in fact, far more vulnerable to local party discontent and challenge, and such challenges are successful in only a small minority of cases. Moreover, not only is the loss of party support uncommon, but, more to the point, its widespread use by a party leader would almost certainly split his party and lead to electoral disaster.

The ultimate power in the hands of the Prime Minister, it is argued, is the power of dissolution, both as a means of bringing dissident MPs into line and, more importantly, of retaining power through a General Election. As a threat to the position of individual MPs, dissolution looms largest for those who hold marginal seats for whom an election in unfavourable circumstances spells almost certain defeat; but a dissolution holds no personal fears for dissident MPs with safe seats and there is no evidence that dissidents hold a disproportionate number of marginal seats. Thus, when Harold Wilson claimed, in the speech quoted above, that the Government 'has a right of appeal to the country for a fresh mandate with supporters who can be counted upon to support the government,'[16] he was dealing largely in political rhetoric rather than political reality. However, dissolution is a more serious threat to the Government that dissident MPs generally support and parliamentary rebels invariably stop short of risking its defeat in Parliament, much as they may dislike some of its policies. In fact, parliamentary rebellions are often carefully managed precisely to avoid endangering the political life of the Government and a dissolution of Parliament in unfavourable circumstances. For example, during the Labour Government of 1966–70, which had a substantial majority in the House of Commons, the number of rebel MPs on various issues was always sufficient to make their point and embarrass the Government, but never enough to bring about its fall.

Of much greater importance in the context of the power of the Prime Minister is the use, by the Prime Minister, of the dissolution of Parliament to effect the judicious timing of a General Election. Used skilfully, as it was by Harold Macmillan in 1959 and Harold Wilson in 1966, it can considerably enhance the Prime Minister' personal dominance, but should the Prime Minister miscalculate or merely be the victim of some unforeseen turn of events, then it can spell disaster and the loss of power, as Harold Wilson found in 1970 and Edward Heath in February 1974. There are limits to the electoral and political manipulation open to a British Prime Minister: opinion polls can be stubbornly unkind, the economy cruelly perverse and sufficient of the electorate curiously unpersuaded.

In spite of the various constraints, the Prime Minister is clearly the key and most powerful figure in the British political system. None of the prime ministerial powers discussed are absolute, but none of the constraints necessarily subordinate the Prime Minister to any other person, office or institution within the system. The ultimate constraints are events which, by their very nature, are totally beyond the control of any Prime Minister or any Government, but which may fundamentally affect their fortunes. The discussion thus far, however, has concentrated mainly on the Prime Minister's position within the broader political system, the context within which the Government, the Cabinet and the Prime Minister operate, but no discussion of the role of the Prime Minister can be complete without looking at the relationship between the Prime Minister and the Cabinet, not just in terms of appointment and dismissal, but in the context of the day-to-day operation of government. The real test of prime ministerial government is therefore twofold: first, to what extent does the Prime Minister dominate the day-to-day running of the Government, and, second, to what extent does the Prime Minister dominate the major issues with which a Government is concerned?

Sir Robert Peel was credited with a dominance which falls into the first category, as Sir James Graham, Home Secretary in Peel's Government of 1841–6, eloquently testifies:

> We never had a Minister who was so truly a first Minister as he is. He makes himself felt in every department and is really cognisant of the affairs of each.[17]

This relationship between the Prime Minister and his Cabinet was remarked upon approvingly by William Gladstone, who was Chancellor of the Exchequer in Peel's administration and who later held the office of Prime Minister four times:

> In the perfectly organised administration, such for example as was that of Sir Robert Peel in 1841–6, nothing of great importance is matured, or would even be projected, in any department without his personal cognisance; any weighty business would commonly go to him before being submitted to the Cabinet . . .
>
> . . . nowhere in the wide world does so great a substance cast so small a shadow; nowhere is there a man who has so much power, with so little to show for it in the way of formal title or prerogative.[18]

Whatever may have been possible in the time of Peel, however, seemed less possible to Lord Rosebery, who served in three of Gladstone's Cabinets and was Prime Minister in 1894–5:

> A Prime Minister who is the senior partner in every department as well as president of the whole, who inspires and vibrates through every part, is almost, if not quite, an impossibility.[19]

This view was endorsed by Lord Oxford and Asquith, who was a member of the Cabinet under Gladstone, Rosebery and Sir Henry Campbell-Bannerman, and Prime Minister from 1908 to 1916:

> it is unquestionable that no Prime Minister could now find the

time or energy for such a departmental autocracy as Peel appeared to have exercised.[20]

Nothing that has occurred since Asquith was Prime Minister would change that view: Governments are now responsible for so much and for such highly complex and technical matters that no one person, even with the powers of a modern Prime Minister, can expect to exert a dominant influence over all departments, all policies and all issues. The Prime Minister is at least as busy as any of his Cabinet colleagues: Harold Wilson, for instance, has recorded that in a three month period in 1975 his diary contained no less than 236 commitments, including eleven Cabinet meetings, twenty-four meetings of Cabinet committees and forty-three other ministerial meetings. Excluding Sundays and three days for Christmas, this amounted to an average of three major commitments per day and this did not include unscheduled meetings with ministers or members of his staff. The staff at the disposal of the Prime Minister, even if the Cabinet Office is included, is insufficient to enable a modern Prime Minister to exercise the detailed supervision credited to Peel.

Lord Wilson, as quoted earlier on the role of the Prime Minister, takes the view that the Prime Minister 'must be *au fait* with . . . developments in the work of all main departments', but such an aim falls far short of dominance. Indeed, it would be a matter for concern if the Prime Minister were not *au fait* with the work of Government departments. The evidence of the Crossman and Castle *Diaries* is that the Prime Minister is kept informed and consulted, where appropriate, but much of the detailed formation of policy is in the hands of the departmental minister and the civil servants, as the examination of the working of the Cabinet in Chapter 5 demonstrates.

The Prime Minister's control of the Cabinet agenda and his or her chairmanship of the Cabinet, backed as they are by the authority of position, enable the Prime Minister to exercise a considerable influence over what the Cabinet discusses and what course those discussions take, and the control over membership of Cabinet committees enhances that influence. Nonetheless, it remains a situation of considerable influence rather than absolute control: many matters must be discussed whether the Prime

Minister likes it or not and major issues are not easily thrust aside; at very least a number of the Prime Minister's Cabinet colleagues are too important to ignore, either departmentally or politically or both; and Cabinet committees do as much to spread influence and decision-making as they do to concentrate it in the hands of the Prime Minister.

Lord Home uses the term 'the Prime Minister's agent – his assistant' to describe the position of Cabinet ministers. Since he had used the term before holding the office of Prime Minister, John Mackintosh later asked Lord Home if he still felt it was an appropriate description after having been Prime Minister. Lord Home confirmed that he did. Moreover, Mackintosh also found that fifteen out of the twenty-three members of Lord Home's Cabinet accepted the description, although some 'felt the words "agent", "assistant", were "a little too royal" as one of them put it.'[21] Such a description is not incompatible with the evidence of Chapter 5, however. The operative phrase in Lord Home's statement is 'in a sense' and there is a sense in which ministers are the Prime Minister's agents: the Prime Minister appoints them and may dismiss them; he or she may intervene in any department or policy area; and, notwithstanding ministerial responsibility, they are responsible in practice first to the Prime Minister. There is, however, another key phrase in Lord Home's description: where the Prime Minister favours a particular course of action 'the Cabinet minister concerned would either have to agree, argue it out in Cabinet, or resign'. The first and last options would be consistent with prime ministerial government, but the second would be so only if the Cabinet could be guaranteed always to side with the Prime Minister. There are, of course, well-known instances when the Prime Minister has failed to carry the Cabinet, such as that experienced by Harold Wilson over the reform of industrial relations in 1969,[22] but it can be argued that such instances are merely notable exceptions which serve to prove the general rule of prime ministerial dominance. However, it is not so much a question of whether the Prime Minister always prevails, so much as whether a significant number of matters are argued out in Cabinet.

The evidence of ministerial memoirs, including those of Prime Ministers and of the Crossman and Castle *Diaries*, is that matters are frequently argued out in Cabinet and in its committees. Crossman, in fact, provides a number of examples which not only illustrate the point, but demonstrate that the prime ministerial will does not always prevail:

*July 1965*

> [The Prime Minister] was trying to help Barbara [Castle, Minister of Overseas Development] . . . and planning to get her allocated another £20 million or so and then later to save money by cutting the road programme . . . When he was defeated he tried to pretend he hadn't made the proposal . . .[23]

*January 1967*

> At the Cabinet Committee on Housing . . . I watched Harold once again trying to sweeten the Chancellor [of the Exchequer][24]

*July 1968*

> It was a raging argument [over public expenditure] and Harold tried hard to help Peter Shore [Secretary of State for Economic Affairs].[25]

*April 1970*

> Harold now almost asked the Cabinet whether we should drop it [British Standard Time] . . . Willie Ross, who had passionately opposed BST, now said we ought to wait until the end of the three years. Jim Callaghan and I agreed, so the PM didn't have his way . . .[26]

The Prime Minister is also sensitive to the Cabinet's reaction to his or her actions – Crossman again:

> [The Prime Minister] told me that we should get a White Paper as well as the Radcliffe Report [on D-Notices] before the Cabinet . . . He was still obviously anxious whether the Cabinet would repudiate him and I assured him that from what he described there would be no difficulty in getting Cabinet backing for both documents.[27]

The prime ministerial argument is too often presented as if a state of conflict between the Prime Minister, on the one hand, and the Cabinet, on the other, is the natural order of things. Yet, why should it be? The Prime Minister stands apart from the Cabinet to the extent of appointing its members and chairing its meetings, but *all* members of the Cabinet, including the Prime Minister, are normally members of the same party and much that they do stems from agreement not conflict. Of course the Prime Minister will appoint a number of ministers who are sympathetic with his or her own views, but the Cabinet also includes other politicians powerful in their own right, some of whom may be regarded as potential rivals for the prime ministerial crown. Of course the Prime Minister makes use of his or her power of appointment and dismissal, power over the Cabinet agenda and the right to consult colleagues separately to pursue those policies which the Prime Minister favours, but the very fact that this is a necessary part of the process belies the simplistic situation that the term 'prime ministerial government' suggests.

The Prime Minister sets the tone and style of a Government and provides the main thrust on certain policies, particularly in the economic sphere, and to that extent (and it is a considerable extent), prime ministerial government exists. The Prime Minister has the advantage of being able to take an overview of the Government's policies, but inevitably becomes involved in and also identified with particular policies, such as the resistance to the devaluation of the pound between 1964 and 1967 in the case of Harold Wilson; Britain's entry to the Common Market in the case of Edward Heath; and the control of the money supply in the case of Margaret Thatcher. In pursuing particular policies, however, the Prime Minister needs Cabinet support. A Prime Minister who was frequently at odds with the Cabinet would soon be bereft of leadership and his or her position would become politically untenable. The Prime Minister is part of the governmental system and, even though as such is better placed than any other individual in the system to manipulate it for his or her own ends, the Prime Minister is not its absolute master. In short, the Prime Minister enjoys a dominant position, not an absolute one, and in stressing that position the term 'prime ministerial government' is accurate, but it neglects the real importance of the part played by the Cabinet and its members.

Conversely, the term 'Cabinet government', whilst stressing the importance of the Cabinet, neglects the dominant position of the Prime Minister. Like the Prime Minister, the Cabinet is part of the wider system and needs to be examined within the context of that system, which has already been shown to be complex rather than simple. Much also depends on the personnel involved and there is much truth in Asquith's comment:

> The Office of Prime Minister is what its holder chooses and is able to make of it.[28]

It is not without a certain irony that Asquith's immediate successor, Lloyd George, made a great deal of the office of Prime Minister and did much to reinforce and increase prime ministerial powers. However, Asquith's comment has a wider application in that the personalities of all those involved in the higher echelons of the governmental system play a part in determining how that system functions at any given time. Few Cabinets, for example, are not marked by the existence or an 'inner Cabinet', a small group of senior ministers, who actually or allegedly dominate the Government and its policies. Occasionally such groups achieve formal status, as they did for a while in the Wilson Government of 1966–70, when first a Steering Committee on Economic Policy and then a Parliamentary Committee formed an inner group. Allegations of 'kitchen Cabinets', powerful personal aides and *éminences grises* are also common. Individual ministers acquire reputations as successes or failures as administrators, as political operators and as parliamentary performers; individual civil servants are periodically credited with degrees of influence which exceed those of the ministers they serve. These are not the products of the system, but of those persons who operate the system. That system may be described, but its operation will vary from one Government to another.

To this must be added the further complication that the British system of government is not the product of a grand design conceived at a particular moment in history, but of many hundreds of years of haphazard evolution. Policy formation and decision-making in Britain are not easily reduced, therefore, to simple patterns. Policy is formed and decisions are made at a number of different levels by a number of different people and bodies – a situation which is succinctly summarised by Mackintosh:

> Some decisions are taken by the Premier alone, some in consultation between him and the senior ministers, while others are left to heads of departments, to the full Cabinet, one of the many Cabinet committees, or to the permanent officials. Of these the Cabinet holds the central position because, though it does not often initiate policy or govern in that sense, it is the place where disputes are settled, where major policies are endorsed and where the balance of forces emerges if there is a disagreement. In the end, most decisions have to be reported to the Cabinet and Cabinet Ministers are the only ones who have the right to complain if they have not been informed or consulted. The precise amount of power held by each agency and the use made of the Cabinet depends on the ideas of the Premier and the personnel and the situation with which he has to deal.[29]

It is, therefore, difficult to disagree with Mackintosh when he says:

> There is no single catchphrase that can describe this form of government.[30]

# Notes and references

## Chapter 4 Organisation and Operation

1. *House of Commons Debates*, 24 May 1979, vol. 967, c.*179* written answers.
2. *Ibid*, 10 November 1970, vol. 806, c. 199 oral answers.
3. Barbara Castle, *The Castle Diaries, 1974–76* (Weidenfeld & Nicolson, London, 1980), p. 49, f.1.
4. Patrick Gordon Walker, *The Cabinet*, rev. edn (Fontana, London 1972), Appendix, pp. 173–4.
5. There is some dispute as to when the chief whip first regularly attended throughout Cabinet meetings. Gordon Walker states that the practice dates from 1951 (Gordon Walker, *op. cit.*, p. 104), whereas John Mackintosh puts the date at some time during the Second World War (John P. Mackintosh, *The British Cabinet*, 3rd edn, Stevens, London, 1977, p. 412).
6. R. H. S. Crossman, *The Diaries of a Cabinet Minister* ed. Janet Morgan (Hamish Hamilton & Jonathan Cape, London, 1975–77) (3 vols. ), vol. III, p. 231.
7. Castle, *op. cit.*, p. 248.
8. Gordon Walker, *op. cit.*, p. 24.
9. Crossman, *Diaries*, vol. III, p. 92. See also vol. II, p. 79 and vol. III, pp. 729–30.
10. Castle, *op. cit.*, p. 51.
11. Crossman, *Diaries*, vol. I, p. 346.
12. *Ibid,* vol. I, p. 534.
13. Castle, *op. cit.*, pp. 562–3.
14. Crossman, *op. cit.*, vol. III, pp. 783–4.
15. Castle, *op.cit.*, p. 446.
16. *Ibid*, p. 360.
17. Crossman, *Diaries*, vol. I. p. 47.
18. *Ibid*, vol. III, p. 117.

## Chapter 5 The Cabinet at Work: Case Studies

1. Castle, *The Castle Diaries, 1974–76*, pp. 443–5.
2. Crossman, *Diaries of a Cabinet Minister*, vol. II. p. 617.
3. *Ibid*, vol. I, p. 28.
4. See Malcolm Joel Barnett, *The Politics of Legislation: the Rent Act 1957* (Weidenfeld & Nicolson, 1969).
5. Crossman, *Diaries*, vol. III, pp. 66–7.
6. *Ibid*, vol. III, p. 511.

7. Quoted in David Marquand, *Ramsay Macdonald* (Jonathan Cape, London, 1977), p. 306.
8. Crossman, *Diaries*, vol. III, p. 78.
9. *Ibid*, vol. III, pp. 168, 429, 756.
10. *Ibid*, vol. I, p. 620.
11. *Ibid*, vol. I, p. 200.
12. *Ibid*, vol. III, p. 259.
13. *Ibid*, vol. III, p. 226.
14. *Ibid*, vol. III, p. 246.
15. *Ibid*, vol. III, p. 686.
16. *Ibid*, vol. III, p. 217.
17. *Ibid*, vol. III, p. 733.
18. Mackintosh, *The British Cabinet*, p. 528.

## Chapter 6 Cabinet or Prime Ministerial Government?

1. R. H. S. Crossman, 'Introduction to Walter Bagehot', *The English Constitution* (C. A. Watts, London, 1964), p. 51. First published by Fontana in 1963. An abridged version is reprinted in Anthony King (ed.), *The British Prime Minister: A Reader* (Macmillan, London, 1969), pp. 151–67.
2. Crossman, *Diaries of a Cabinet Minister*, vol. I, p. 11.
3. Janet Morgan (ed.), *The Backbench Diaries of Richard Crossman* (Hamish Hamilton & Jonathan Cape, London, 1981).
4. Published as *Inside View: Three Lectures on Prime Ministerial Government* (Jonathan Cape, London, 1972).
5. Crossman, 'Introduction to Bagehot', p. 54.
6. Crossman, *Diaries*, vol. I, p. 198.
7. John P. Mackintosh, 'The Prime Minister and the Cabinet', *Parliamentary Affairs*, vol. XXI, 1967–8, p. 68. This article is reprinted in King, *op. cit.* pp. 191–210, under the title of 'A Rejoinder'.
8. Mackintosh, *The British Cabinet*, p. 269.
9. John Morley, *Walpole* (Macmillan, London, 1889), p. 157.
10. Sir Anthony Eden (Lord Avon), *Full Circle* (Cassell, London, 1960), p. 269.
11. Sir Alec Douglas-Home (Lord Home) in *The Observer*, 23 August 1961, quoted in Mackintosh, *The British Cabinet*, pp. 628–9.
12. Sir Harold Wilson, *The Labour Government 1964–1970: A Personal Record* (Weidenfeld & Nicolson and Michael Joseph, London, 1971), p. 45.
13. Crossman, *Diaries*, vol. I, pp. 11–12.
14. *The Times*, 3 March 1967.
15. Wilson, *op. cit.*, p. 378.

16. *The Times*, 3 March 1967.

17. Quoted in John Morley, *Life of Gladstone* (Macmillan, London, 1903), vol. I, p. 248.

18. W. E. Gladstone, *Gleanings of Past Years* (John Murray, London, 1879), vol. I, pp. 243, 244.

19. Quoted in Lord Oxford and Asquith, *Fifty Years of Parliament* (Cassell, London, 1926), vol. II, p. 185.

20. *Ibid*, p. 186.

21. Mackintosh, 'The Prime Minister and the Cabinet', p. 67, f. 27.

22. See Peter Jenkins, *The Battle of Downing Street* (Knight, London, 1970).

23. Crossman, *Diaries*, vol. I, p. 282.

24. *Ibid*, vol. II, p. 205.

25. *Ibid*, vol. III, p. 123.

26. *Ibid*, vol. III, p. 897.

27. *Ibid*, vol. II, p. 379.

28. Asquith, *op. cit.*, vol. II, p. 185.

29. Mackintosh, *The British Cabinet*, pp. 541–2.

30. *Ibid*, p. 543.

# Select Bibliography

It has been an important part of the argument in this book that the Cabinet is not an isolated institution, but one whose operation can be fully understood only in the context of its role as part of the policy-forming process. This means that not only is it important to view the Cabinet in its wider institutional setting, but even more so to see it in the context of day-to-day politics. This is best achieved by observing the operation of the Cabinet through current political issues and events by following these in the press, radio and television. Newspapers, especially *The Times, Guardian, Daily Telegraph, Sunday Times*, the *Observer* and the *Sunday Telegraph*, provide an invaluable running commentary on political issues and events. Periodicals, such as the *Economist*, the *New Statesman* and the *Spectator*, provide analysis and comment in greater depth. Apart from some Open University programmes, particularly in the course 'Decision-Making in Britain', there are no television or radio programmes which deal regularly with the work and operation of the Cabinet, but there are, of course, a number of current affairs programmes which are highly relevant. These include the BBC's 'Panorama', 'Newsnight' and 'Newsweek' and ITV's 'World in Action', 'TV Eye' and 'Weekend World'. In addition, the regular radio programmes 'Today in Parliament', 'Yesterday in Parliament', 'Inside Parliament' and 'The Week in Westminster' are useful, especially now that extracts from parliamentary debates are broadcast.

One of the most illuminating television programmes, however, was the fictional comedy series 'Yes Minister', some of the scripts of which have since been published in the form of a mock Crossman-style diary (Jonathan Lynn and Antony Jay (eds), *Yes Minister. The Diaries of a Cabinet Minister by the Rt Hon. James Hacker, MP* (BBC Publications, 1981). Although 'Yes Minister' is intended to amuse and entertain, it is by no means divorced from the reality of political life and offers a great deal of insight into the role of the minister and his or her relationship with civil servants. There are also a number of academic journals which regularly contain relevant articles including *Parliamentary Affairs, Political Quarterly, Public Administration* and *Public Law*.

Because the Cabinet is a central institution of British government it is important to consider reading on the wider political and constitutional context, as well as more specialised works. There are a great variety of general texts on British politics and much depends on the needs and tastes of the individual reader. Although textbooks inevitably get out of date (some more rapidly than others depending on the speed and nature of events) this should not deter the reader from consulting or necessarily purchasing textbooks published more than a year or two ago. John P. Mackintosh, *The Government and Politics of Britain*, revised and updated by Peter G. Richards (Hutchinson, 4th edn, 1982); A. H. Hanson and Malcolm Walles, *Governing Britain* (Fontana, 3rd edn, 1980); A. H. Birch, *The British System of Government*, Allen and Unwin, 4th edn, 1980); and Michael Rush, *Parliamentary Government in Britain* (Pitman, 1981) provide useful general surveys. A more exhaustive account can be found in R. M. Punnett, *British Government and Politics* (Heinemann, 4th edn, 1980).

There are a number of standard texts on constitutional history, such as Sir D. L. Keir, *The Constitutional History of Modern Britain* (A. and C. Black, 1964) and S. B. Chrimes, *English Constitutional History* (Oxford University Press, 1965). In addition textbooks on constitutional law, such as O. Hood Phillips and Paul Jackson, *Constitutional and Administrative Law*, (Sweet and Maxwell, 6th edn, 1978) and E. C. S. Wade and G. G. Phillips, *Constitutional Law* (Longman, 9th edn, 1977), provide useful legal background.

G. Marshall and G. C. Moodie, *Some Problems of the Constitution* (Hutchinson, 1961); H. J. Laski, *Parliamentary Government in England* (Allen and Unwin, 1958); H. J. Laski, *Reflections on the Constitution* (Manchester University Press, 1962); L. S. Amery, *Thoughts on the Constitution* (Oxford University Press, 1964); Ian Gilmour, *The Body Politic* (Hutchinson, 1969); and, Max Nicholson, *The System* (Hodder and Stoughton, 1967), are stimulating commentaries on the British constitution and political system.

There are also a large number of more specialised textbooks available which deal with the wider aspects of British politics relevant to the role and operation of the Cabinet. For example, A. H. Birch, *Representative and Responsible Government* (Allen and Unwin, 1964) offers a wideranging discussion of the basic ideas underlying the constitution, and a more polemical view can be found in Nevil Johnson, *In Search of the Constitution* (Pergamon, 1977 and Methuen, 1980); J. J. Richardson, *The Policy-Making Process* (Routledge and Kegan Paul, 1969) provides a general account of policy-formation in Britain, whilst R. G. S. Brown and David R. Steel, *The Administrative Process in Britain* (Methuen, 2nd edn, 1979) is a useful account of the development and operation of the Civil Service; S. A. Walkland, *The Legislative Process in Britain* (Allen and Unwin, 1968) provides an admirable description and discussion of Parliament's role in policy formation, whilst Michael Rush, *Parliament and the Public* (Longman, 1976) offers a wider view of the role of Parliament; Richard Rose, *The Problem of Party Government*

(Macmillan, 1974) is probably the best discussion of the role and operation of parties in British politics.

The major contemporary book on the Cabinet is John P. Mackintosh, *The British Cabinet* (Stevens, 3rd edn, 1977). This standard work was originally commissioned as a revised version of A. B. Keith's *The British Cabinet System* (first published in 1936), by N. H. Gibbs (Stevens, 2nd edn, 1952), but Mackintosh decided that a totally new book was necessary. Mackintosh gives a detailed account of the origins and development of the Cabinet and then uses this as a basis for discussing the operation of the modern Cabinet and the role of the Prime Minister. Sir Ivor Jennings, *Cabinet Government* (Cambridge University Press, 3rd edn, 1959) was also a standard work, but was less systematically historical in its treatment and inevitably less up to date than Mackintosh. Nonetheless, Jennings is an extremely scholarly account of the operation of the Cabinet system and the role of the Prime Minister and includes a number of useful appendices, one of which contains brief biographical notes on leading politicians of the late nineteenth and early twentieth centuries. An excellent short account and discussion of the operation of the Cabinet, which draws upon the author's own experience as a Cabinet minister, can be found in Patrick Gordon Walker, *The Cabinet* (first published in 1970) (Fontana, rev. edn, 1972). The book includes Gordon Walker's view of the 'Cabinet government-prime ministerial government' debate. Hans Daalder, *Cabinet Reform in Britain, 1914–1963* (Oxford University Press, 1964) is a more specialised account of the development of the Cabinet since the outbreak of the First World War. A useful collection of articles is published in V. Herman and J. Alt (eds), *Cabinet Studies: A Reader* (Macmillan, 1975) and Bruce Headey, *British Cabinet Ministers* (Allen and Unwin, 1974) is a valuable study of the backgrounds and careers of ministers.

There are relatively few books dealing with particular aspects of the role and operation of the Cabinet. R. K. Mosley, *The Story of the Cabinet Office* (Routledge and Kegan Paul, 1969) is useful, but limited on developments since 1945 because of the operation of the thirty year rule on access to Cabinet papers. Joel Barnett, *Inside the Treasury* (André Deutsch, 1982) provides a fascinating account of the role of the Chief Secretary to the Treasury in dealing with public expenditure, reinforced by the authority of a former holder of the post. William Keegan and R. Pennant-Rea, *Who Runs the Economy? – Control and Influence in British Economic Planning* (Maurice Temple Smith, 1979) is a readable account and discussion of the wider formation of economic policy.

Apart from memoirs, a number of politicians have provided useful insights into the inner workings of government in Britain. In the 1950s, for example, Herbert (later Lord) Morrison was persuaded to write a politician's eye-view of British government in *Government and Parliament* (Oxford University Press, 3rd edn, 1964). More recently the former Prime Minister, Sir Harold Wilson, published an idiosyncratic but useful account of the workings of the Government in general and the Cabinet in particular in *The Governance of Britain* (Weidenfeld and Nicolson and Michael Joseph, 1976, and Sphere Books, 1977). Harold Wilson also published his thoughts on various matters relevant to the Cabinet *before* becoming Prime Minister in *Whitehall and Beyond* (BBC Publications, 1964). Jeremy Bray, a former non-Cabinet minister, has written a detailed account and discussion of how decisions are made in the British governmental system in *Decision in Government* (Gollancz, 1969) and five former Labour Cabinet ministers – Tony Benn, Edmund Dell, Merlyn Rees, William Rodgers and Shirley Williams – gave their views on the matter in *Policy and Practice: The Experience of Government* (Royal Institute of Public Administration, 1980).

Memoirs are, of course, a major source of information about the operation of the Cabinet, but the most useful 'memoir-type' sources are the published diaries of two former Labour Cabinet ministers, Richard Crossman and Barbara Castle. R. H. S. Crossman, *The Diaries of a Cabinet Minister* (3 vols ) (Hamish Hamilton and Jonathan Cape, 1975–7) provide a detailed, day-by-day account of the operation of government seen through the eyes of one of the senior members of the Labour Government of 1964–70. The *Diaries* include accounts of meetings of the Cabinet and its committees and informal meetings and discussions with ministerial colleagues, civil servants and other. Barbara Castle, *The Castle Diaries, 1974–76* (Weidenfeld and Nicolson, 1980) is a similar volume covering the period of the Labour Government 1974–6. Neither diarist attempts a systematic analysis of the working of the Cabinet or the wider machinery of government, although from time to time Crossman usefully digresses into discussions of the roles of the Cabinet and the Prime Minister, the relationship between ministers and civil servants and so on, whereas Barbara Castle concentrates more exclusively on policy matters. Nonetheless, both provide first-hand accounts written soon after the events they describe and are an invaluable insight into the whole operation of British government.

Ministerial memoirs abound and only a few of the more recent and relevant ones can be mentioned here. They lack the immediacy of the Crossman and Castle diaries, but they still constitute an important source of information and opinion. With the important exception of Sir Winston Churchill, all postwar Prime Ministers between 1945 and 1976 have published memoirs. Churchill, of course, wrote his account of the Second

World War (6 vols) (Cassell, 1948–54) and this, *inter alia*, deals with the operation of the 1940–5 War Cabinet. Fortunately, a detailed and highly scholarly account of the postwar Churchill Government of 1951–5 can be found in Anthony Seldon, *Churchill's Indian Summer: The Conservative Government, 1951–55* (Hodder and Stoughton, 1981). The various volumes of prime ministerial memoirs are as follows: Clement (later Earl) Attlee, *As It Happened* (Heinemann, 1954); Francis Williams, *A Prime Minister Remembers: The War and Postwar Memoirs of Earl Attlee* (Heinemann, 1961); Sir Anthony Eden (later the Earl of Avon), *Memoirs: Full Circle; Facing the Dictators*; and *The Reckoning* (3 vols) (Cassell, 1960, 1962 and 1965); Harold Macmillan, *Memoirs* (6 vols.) Macmillan, 1966–73); Sir Alec Douglas-Home (Lord Home), *The Way the Wind Blows* (Collins, 1976) and *Border Airs* (Collins, 1979); Sir Harold Wilson, *The Labour Government, 1964–70: A Personal Record* (Weidenfeld and Nicolson and Michael Joseph, 1971) and *Final Term: The Labour Government, 1974–76* (Weidenfeld and Nicolson and Michael Joseph, 1979).

Among former ministers who have written memoirs are, on the Conservative side, The Earl of Kilmuir (Sir David Maxwell-Fyfe), *Political Adventure* (Weidenfeld and Nicolson, 1964); Lord Hill of Luton, *Both Sides of the Hill: The Memoirs of Charles Hill* (Heinemann, 1964); R. A. (the late Lord) Butler, *The Art of the Possible* (Hamish Hamilton, 1971); and Reginald Maudling, *Memoirs* (Sidgwick and Jackson, 1978). On the Labour side, George Brown (now Lord George-Brown), *In My Way* (Gollancz, 1971); George (now Lord) Wigg, *George Wigg* (Michael Joseph, 1972) and Douglas Jay, *Change and Fortune* (Hutchinson, 1980).

A number of prime ministerial aides have also written memoirs or accounts of the operation of government. For example, Harold Wilson's former Political Secretary, Marcia Williams (now Lady Falkender) has published her account of life at the political centre in *Inside No 10* (Weidenfeld and Nicolson, 1972) and Joe Haines, Press Secretary to Harold Wilson from 1969 to 1976, relates his experiences in *The Politics of Power* (Jonathan Cape, 1977). On the Conservative side, John Colville, former secretary to Winston Churchill – and later to Attlee – *Footprints in Time* (Collins, 1976); Lord Egremont (John Wyndham), former secretary to Harold Macmillan, *Wyndham and Children First* (Macmillan, 1968); and Sir Harold Evans, former Press Secretary to Harold Macmillan, *Downing Street Diary: The Macmillan Years, 1957–63* (Hodder Stoughton, 1981) are less controversial, but interesting nonetheless.

The role of the Prime Minister is the subject of a number of books. One of the most useful is Anthony King (ed.), *The British Prime Minister:*

*A Reader* (Macmillan, 1969), which consists of a collection of articles on the position and role of the Prime Minister, including some American comparisons, and the major contributions on the 'Cabinet government – prime ministerial government' debate. This debate is also very much to the fore in F. W. G. Benemy, *The Elected Monarch* (Harrap, 1965) and Humphrey Berkeley, *The Power of the Prime Minister* (Allen and Unwin, 1968). However, the classic statement of the prime ministerial government case is found in Richard Crossman's introduction to a new edition of Walter Bagehot, *The English Constitution* (Fontana, 1963), republished by C. A. Watts, with a bibliography and index, 1964. Bagehot's book was originally published as a series of essays in the magazine *The Fortnightly* and was then published in book form in 1867. It is a classic account of the operation of the British system of government in the middle of the nineteenth century, arguing that the Cabinet is the crucial political institution and the pivot of the political system.

*The English Constitution* also contains an interesting nineteenth-century comparison with and criticism of the American presidential system. An early twentieth-century view of British government in general, and the role of the Cabinet in particular, can be found in A. Lawrence Lowell, *The Government of England* (2 vols) originally published in 1908 (Macmillan, new edn 1926). In his introduction to Bagehot Crossman develops Bagehot's concept of the 'dignified' and 'efficient' parts of the political system to support his argument that Britain has prime ministerial rather than Cabinet government. Crossman's views can be found at greater length in *Inside View: Three Lectures on Prime Ministerial Government* (Jonathan Cape, 1972), which draws upon his experience as a member of the Labour Cabinet between 1964 and 1970.

Relevant information and data on British government generally and the membership of Governments in particular (including the Cabinet) can be found in Chris Cook and Brendan Keith, *British Historical Facts, 1830–1900* (Macmillan, 1975) and David Butler and Anne Sloman, *British Political Facts, 1900–1979* (Macmillan, 1980).

# Index